Best wishes,

My Closing Arguments

A Texas Lawyer's Life

by Fred Parks

Edited by Mickey Herskowitz

This book is dedicated to —

My mother, Nora Parks Hubbard

My wife, Mabel Roberson Parks

My daughter, Judy Stauffer

A future lawyer poses — thumb in belt, one hand on the rail.

Contents

Foreword

The greatest and most difficult challenge in my life was the self-created one of becoming a respected and competent attorney.

To achieve my goal, the first hurdle I faced was to be admitted to law school and then to graduate. This was no simple task for me. I was lacking in any pre-law preparation.

After an aborted attempt to go from high school into law school, I backed up and enrolled as a freshman at Rice Institute. Health problems caused me to drop out of Rice.

Again, I started over and earned my degree from the South Texas School of Law. I was admitted to the Texas bar in 1937. I knew at the outset that my personal mission was to be recognized as an honest lawyer, with a reputation for being able to handle difficult cases.

Any success others may attribute to my practice of law, I can say with no false modesty, was the result of help I received from litigators far more accomplished than I. The earliest help came in my first five years of practice as an associate with the small firm of Burris and Benton. Neither of these men had a fondness for the rigors of the courtroom. Thus, when I joined them, their backlog of cases became my immediate responsibility.

I struggled and made daily mistakes as I "worked" the firm's cases. In the process, I developed my own courtroom techniques, blending them with a few I borrowed from others. I am indebted to all who helped and preceded me — they made me the lawyer I became.

Additionally, during a portion of my twenty months of service during World War II, I acted as the Judge Advocate for the 15th Air Force in Italy, during which time I tried court martial and war crime cases.

Gradually, over time, I feel my mission was fulfilled, and most importantly without resorting to practices I have always abhorred.

I am part of a generation whose ranks are thinning, hardened by the Great Depression and tempered by war. The money I made from the practice of law enabled me to branch out, invest in other businesses and develop a taste for fine things. I have led a life I could not have imagined, as a young boy born in the Indian Territory.

Acknowledgment

Writing a memoir is not unlike trying a lawsuit. There are many contributors in unseen roles, and they need to be noted and thanked.

First among them is my friend, Hunter L. Martin, Jr., who has helped me in many ways through the years. In the development of this book, he was a valued advisor and critic and source of information.

Virginia McClintock transcribed countless hours of dictation, and kept the files and the manuscript, as it grew, in always impeccable order. John Furnace and Beverly Marules, members of my loyal and supportive staff, helped keep the office, and this project, moving.

To Mickey Herskowitz, a nationally known author, who organized and shaped this material, goes my deepest gratitude for his efforts and patience.

Section I

The Early Years
July 1906 to May 1925

At age thirteen, with mother, Nora Parks Hubbard.

Chapter 1

Out of Oklahoma

LIFE WAS A STRUGGLE in the Indian Territory. Thus, it seemed only fitting that I should be born there, on the 9th of July, in the year 1906. Fitting because — if any one word would describe my life for several decades — "struggle" was as accurate as any.

Yet at the turn of the Twentieth Century, great and sweeping events were taking place that would forever rearrange the world. In 1901, the discovery of oil at Spindletop, a marshy area near the town of Beaumont, Texas, marked the beginning of the liquid fuel age. In 1902, Henry Ford founded his own company to make automobiles. In 1903, the Wright Brothers made their famous flight at Kittyhawk. That year the first male motion picture star made his debut in "The Great Train Robbery." He was known as Bronco Billy, but his real name was Max Aronson.

In 1904, rights to the Panama Canal were transferred to the United States. (That same year, a woman was arrested for smoking a cigarette in an open car in New York City. The outcome of the case is unrecorded.) In 1905, President Theodore Roosevelt used the growing prestige of the U. S. to persuade Russia and Japan to end their hostilities. And the Pennsylvania Railroad established the fastest, long-distance train service in the world, 18 hours between New York and Chicago.

World or national news had little impact on that vast patch of land then called the Indian Territory. It was renamed Oklahoma and admitted to the Union as the 46th state the year after my birth. Inventions and global adventures rated far down on a scale that began with survival.

Indian Territory. The phrase evoked a culture of horses and open range and the last frontier. I was born 40 years after the Civil War ended and Lincoln was assassinated; 30 years after Custer and all his troops died at Little Bighorn. This was history close by.

I believe I was blessed to be born when I was, able to watch the full flowering of the American century. I lived through two World Wars, serving in one of them, and the Great Depression. As a boy, who could have foreseen what the wonders of science and the imagination of man would bring? Jet aircraft, rockets blasting into space and astronauts walking on the moon; microwaves, lasers, computers that talk to us, heart transplants, babies in a tube, were wonders yet to come.

In the early 1900's, travel was slow and difficult over roads that were little more than trails, if they existed at all. Most people lived hand-to-mouth, bought food and clothes on credit, and dreamed of owning land and a home. Hardship was a strict teacher. Lessons learned were not soon forgotten.

I was born in Oklahoma City, the only child of Nora and John Parks. My father was a drifter who helped build and paint houses and later smoke stacks. Wages were minimal and I do not remember ever having more than the bare essentials. My father was not a factor in my existence. Shortly after my birth, he left my mother alone to provide for herself and her son. A plump little woman who never raised her voice, I knew that whatever the situation, she worked hard to feed us.

She did so with as much help as our neighbors, John and Scotty Rice, could provide. They were Aunt Scotty and Uncle John to me, although they were unrelated to us except in the way that common deprivation can bring people together.

With statehood, conditions in Oklahoma actually grew more severe. Small farmers had to contend with thin soil, boll weevils, grand weather dramas — rain and heat and dust storms — and the greed of merchants and landlords. Still, the settlers came. And they came. And they came.

The Rices and Mother were pioneers, who together made the Kickapoo country "races" which were extensively advertised for those daring to stake out a claim on one of America's last frontiers. The Kickapoos were among the tribes the federal government dumped on Oklahoma after the Five Civilized Tribes were resettled in 1830, at the end of what the Cherokees called "The Trail of Tears."

The original land rush in April of 1889 drew the first wave of homesteaders. The railroads, mining and lumber camps and trail drives eroded the way of life the tribes had known. But even as settlers dug in for the long haul, the Indian Territory was hospitable to those passing by — a long line of outlaws that included the James Gang, the Youngers, the Daltons, Ned Christie, Belle Starr and Wyatt Earp, before he went straight. Young boys grew up listening to the stories of those gunslingers and bank robbers.

It all came together in a nearly mythic time and place. To own land was to be independent, if not rich. The land runs gave birth to a category of people, "Sooners," who would enter the territory early, hide in a gully, and when the starting gun sounded jump out and stake their claims. (The name Kickapoo was given an additional exposure when the cartoonist, Al Capp, referred in his Li'l Abner comic strip to a high-octane beverage as "Kickapoo Joy Juice.")

As a small boy, in 1912, I couldn't fully appreciate the historic nature of these last scrambles for free or cheap land. My excitement was that of one taking part in any horse-and-buggy race. The Rices had inspected the area that would be open to the wagons, and had picked out what they believed to be good farmland. At the crack of the pistol, they headed for their hoped-for homestead with all of the fury necessary to arrive before the nearest competitor. Mother made the mad dash with Aunt Scotty and Uncle John. They drove a stake into the ground and rode back to the land office to claim their tract.

It was in every respect risky business. There was the promise of land, but no promise that crops would grow. The life was physically demanding. It took years just to break the sod and plant a few acres of corn and wheat. They had only the crudest implements, an axe, a hoe, a shovel, with which to work the land.

There were several land runs between 1889 and 1913. An account of one survives in western literature, as told by a plowhand named Billy McGinty, who left West Texas to find his stake in the Cherokee Strip:

"I've seen many a danged thing happen in Oklahoma . . . But, nothing, nowhere, compares with that big stampede back there in 1893 — a thousand pawing, bellowing humans tearing out at the pop of a gun to lay claim to six hundred million acres. In all my days of riding, I never rode harder . . . than I did in that one hour. I reckon there's no sound louder than that of the smashing wheels and the pounding hoofs of that 'git-there-first' race into the Cherokee Strip . . .

"I had already slipped over into the strip and picked out the place I aimed to file on. A hundred and sixty acres on the bank of Camp Creek; land sloping down so pretty you could run furrows . . . smooth and straight as ribbons. I'd sow and reap money. Then I'd find me a spry girl and raise myself a crop of kids on that stretch . . .

"Day of the Run, I beat the roosters up. By eight o'clock, four hours till starting time, men and horses were packed in so close lightning couldn't have cut them loose. Behind the saddles were the wheels; five miles of 'em waiting to tear out into that Promised Land. I saw every contraption that's rolled since Noah put rubber tires on the Ark.

" . . . One shot in the air. Wheels cracked! Whips

7

popped! Hoofs thundered! The Run was on. Horse's hides were raw red from being whipped to make them run faster. Drivers were standing up in wagons and buggies, lashing their own teams and those of other men when they crowded too close. Just before we reached the creek, I jumped off at the stretch I had picked out.

"I grabbed rocks and sticks to mark off my hundred and sixty ... I cut a branch from a cottonwood and stuck my bandana on it. For the law said you had to put up some kind of a banner when you had finished staking a place ...

"Then I stood up and looked out over that first piece of ground that I had ever called my own. 'You're somebody now, Billy,' I said to myself."

That would have been a poetic ending, if the story had ended there. But it did not. McGinty lost his land to a claim jumper.

I don't want to put too fine a point on this, but in a small corner of my soul I feel a kinship with Billy McGinty. I have gone through life, more often than not, as if I were involved in the last land rush. And if I have had my claim jumped, a time or two, I've surely won my share.

Most of my early years were spent moving from town to town, while Mother looked for a better job or lighter burdens. By the time I was old enough for grade school, we had moved to Wichita, Kansas. We lived there, in a rented house at 311 Riverview, from 1913 to 1919. In those days, Wichita was the kind of town where the three most important places were the country store, the church and the barbershop.

My mother had made arrangements with the barber to cut my hair on a regular basis, and she would pay him later. On one occasion, because it was the style or a fad, I asked him to shave my head. He asked if it was okay with my mother and I lied and said, yes. He shaved my hair and I really caught hell when I got home.

I also pulled a George Washington reversal. I picked the fruit off a neighbor's tree and lied about it. When I finally admitted my misdeed to my mother, her punishment was swift and stern. As a result of the swats I received, that episode has stayed with me to this day.

I watched my mother toil at the hardest and lowest kind of labor. She worked as a servant, swept out a factory, worked long hours in a laundry sorting the clothes by hand as they came through the wringer. I never heard her complain. She concealed her disappointment when anything went wrong, or she could not give us some simple fact of life. The teachings I received from her stood me in good stead when I, in turn, had little or nothing to eat and no place to sleep. During the dry times, including a long spell in Houston, her example let me keep my hopes up.

In Wichita every cent counted, and soon I joined her on the work force. I had a paper route delivering the Wichita Beacon. Within a week, I was hounding the manager for a second route. He refused, saying that no youngster could handle two. Finally, he gave me the second route to shut me up. I handled the double duties with such ease that one day he insisted on going along when I delivered the papers to see how I did it. The answer was simple enough. I used roller skates, skating down the middle of the street, trying to hit the porches on either side. It didn't much matter if my aim was true or not, so long as the paper reached the right house. By using roller skates, I covered twice the distance in half the time. The other boys walked from house to house, walking up one side of the street and crossing to the other, to toss their papers one at a time.

At one point, I earned 25 cents a day working for a huckster, plus whatever I could eat off the wagon. The owner bought his produce from a wholesaler and hired two boys to take the cart through certain routes of the city each day. We carried a basket from door to door and told the lady of the house what fruits and vegetables we had that day. She would either slam the door in our faces or walk out to the wagon to make her purchases.

We worked from daylight until dark, and I studied the huckster when he purchased, say, a case of strawberries. Before he left the wholesale house, he would take the individual boxes, shake them up and take a few berries off the top of each box. By doing this, he would have a case, plus three or four extra boxes.

I worked as if I were twins and always the incentive was money. As one humorist said, money is something you need in case you don't die. But in the beginning, I saw my odd jobs as a way to make myself the equal of the boys on a budget from their families.

Pleasures were few and simple. One job mother had was in a plant that manufactured candy. When she had pennies to spare, she bought pieces of candy swept up from the factory floor, bagged and sold.

They kept the floors clean and gathered the candy gently, to shake the dirt out. So it wasn't a bad deal.

During school vacations, when I wasn't working — which wasn't often — she rewarded me with a dime. With that financing, I would drop by Wonderland Park, rent a swimsuit and swim all day, if I wanted. For the same dime, you could take a steam bath, too. I was nine or ten years old, given to catching colds in the winter, and not too robust. But I was learning that I had some athletic talent. At the pool, I could take a pair of trapeze rings and, like the men in the circus, throw my shoulders out of joint, swing back and forth, then turn over and dive off the board.

While living in Wichita, Mother remarried. Frank Hubbard, originally from South Dakota, came from a large farming family. In 1919, the three of us headed for Presho, a community of no more than five hundred people. I remember attending a Hubbard family reunion with eighty to ninety members present.

My stepfather's brother was mayor of Presho and one of the town's more affluent residents. Along with practically the entire population, he made his living from raising hay. That summer, of 1919, I worked on the hay harvest. Aside from that activity, there was little else to do in Presho. Thus, Mother and her new husband decided that she and I would travel to Tulsa, where Aunt Scotty and Uncle John Rice had a job waiting for her. Frank Hubbard stayed behind in South Dakota.

Our stay in Tulsa stretched into two years — my seventh and eighth grades in school. School was in a small, temporary wooden building and, in the wintertime, the ingenuity of the kids would go to work. When the teacher was out of the room, we would open the windows and doors because, if the temperature dropped below a certain level, school would be dismissed. This worked for awhile, until the teacher caught on.

In much of America it was a lilac time just after the First World War and before the Depression choked the country. In cities like New York and Chicago and St. Louis, it was a time of gaslights and high starched collars and no Social Security.

But most of my memories of Tulsa were work and weather-related. I once witnessed the odd havoc of a tornado — strands of straw driven like spikes into a tree trunk.

One of my jobs was picking pecans up in Turkey Mountain, across the Arkansas River on Tulsa's west side. I sold them to the men at the Cosden Refinery on the way back to town. War restrictions were still enforced and no one was permitted to enter the refinery, so I made my sales through the wire fence.

In Tulsa, Charles Page, a prominent oilman, owned the hotel near the rooming house where my mother and I lived. The hotel was reserved for working mothers, and single women looking for work, and no men were allowed in the units.

I was befriended by a repairman for the Otis Elevator Company, and one Saturday he invited me to go with him on a call. An elevator was an attraction in those days, about as close to high technology as it got.

To fix a problem, he had to take off the ground plates (they were on the street) and a small crowd quickly gathered to watch him, myself included.

He had to trace the various colored wires and, first, he had to wipe off the grease so he could tell what the colors were. It was a difficult job and an elderly man — at least, he was gray-haired and elderly to me — began to offer advice.

"Mister," the repairman said, "I've been trained and I'm getting paid to do this job and I think you ought to stand back and let me get on with it." The older man then walked off.

Someone in the crowd asked the technician if he knew who the man was. He said he didn't know and didn't care. The onlooker said, "Well, you ought to care because that was Charles Page and he owns this office building."

In due course, Mr. Page returned and joined the crowd still watching the work in progress. He finally spoke up and said, "Young man, you were absolutely right in telling me that you are the expert, not I. Notwithstanding the fact that I own this building, you are the one I hired to fix my elevator. If I had known how to repair it, I would not have had to call on you." He tipped his hat and again walked away. I thought that was the mark of a gentleman.

Mr. Page also qualified as something rare even today and almost unknown then — a humanitarian. He adopted underprivileged youngsters in order to help them get an education. I never knew if he became aware of me, or if my mother sought him out, but at one point she considered putting me up for adoption. I had grave misgivings about leaving her, but she explained that I would have "advantages" she could never give me — proper clothes and food and a chance to go to college. She said she would still be able to see me. I felt no sense of loss when the arrangement, for whatever reason, failed to go through.

In Tulsa, my mother worked in a Swift's packing plant, picking chickens, and I worked with her during the summer. They paid five cents a bird. A cent and a half of that went to the so-called "rougher," who killed the chickens and plucked the heavy feathers. The remainder went to the person who finished the picking.

The finishers would hang the chicken on a rotating table, and if it passed inspection your tag was pinned on the leg. At the end of the day, the tags were used to count the number of chickens you had picked so you could be paid. It was slow, nasty work and not very pretty.

(Over the years, the best lawyers learn to use all of life's experiences. I suppose I can look back and say that plucking chickens is not bad training for examining a witness.)

When we had saved enough money to return to South Dakota, there was serious discussion between my mother and stepfather as to whether we should go by prairie schooner or by train. In the end, it was cheaper to buy two train tickets than a team of horses.

For those under, say, fifty or so, it must be difficult to understand what the railroad once meant to this country. Not just in the movement of people, or the territories it opened, but as a romantic symbol of an age that once was and will never be again. Oh, sure, we still have trains today, but Amtrak doesn't wave as well or toot as loudly when it goes by.

Most of my early memories of the railroad are of people milling around the platform and dozing on the benches. Folks would flock to the station when they heard the whistle of an arriving train, just to see who got off and who was leaving.

Part of the pleasure of hanging around the railroad depot was watching, and hearing, the operator tap out his messages in Morse code. They were the first to know about floods and election results and major crime stories. During the World Series, they would post the score by innings on a blackboard. By late afternoon maybe two hundred people would be standing there, watching the numbers go up, *seeing* the game.

But as so often with the institutions that invite our nostalgia, train travel was not all that romantic in the 1920's. There was no first class and no dining car. You just took a seat and when the train stopped, you would get off and eat at the Harvey House. (Long after I was established as an attorney, there was a Harvey House near the railroad station in Houston, on Texas Avenue.)

You would have just enough time to eat and then the whistle blew and you had to climb back aboard. I distinctly remember tasting my first beer in Kansas City, Missouri, when the train stopped for lunch at the Harvey House. I asked my mother if I could order a beer, and was given a small glass to drink. This was the first alcoholic beverage I ever tasted. I was probably fifteen.

I had no strong emotions, either way, about returning to South Dakota. It was a scenic place, and those who lived there were a hardy stock. But the state was without charm or distinction, except for its role in World War I. It was crucial to the war effort, for a reason that will date us all. South Dakota was probably the country's main supplier of hay, without which the army's horses and mules would go unfed.

During the war, most of the hay produced in Presho was shipped in government containers to the front. The restrictions were so strict that from the time you cut and baled the grass, no rain could touch the shipment. Any hay that got wet was rejected by the government and had to be sold elsewhere.

One year, the family rented a farm adjacent to the Rosebud Indian Reservation, some ten miles from Presho. Mr. Hubbard acquired horses and some machinery, grazed a few cows and went into the hay business himself. In the winters, on weekends and holidays, I hauled 100-pound bales of hay on a flatbed wagon, which could be piled and secured in such a way as to tie down the load, which weighed a total of around seven tons. I went out with a team of four horses, loaded the hay and brought it back to town.

It was while performing these tasks that I experienced how satisfying and easy it would be to freeze to death. The signs are that you begin to feel sleepy and very comfortable. You want to lie down and doze off. When this would occur, you had to get off the wagon, walk behind the moving wheels and exercise until you overcame this condition.

Winters in South Dakota could be brutal. On one occasion, for a period of some ten days and nights, the temperature never got above thirty degrees below zero. I have seen it so cold that you could take a pail of hot water and throw it into the air, and before it hit the ground it would be slush.

Some of the worst blizzards I can remember occurred when it was not snowing. The snow would be so dry you couldn't even make a snowball. Then the wind would blow the dry air so hard you could not see your hand in front of your face. You could look up and see the blue sky above.

I know of one lady who froze to death going from her house to the woodshed for firewood. She became disoriented and lost her way in that short distance. Most of the people would have a rope stretched from the backdoor to the woodshed to the barn. As they went from one to the other, they held onto the rope. If you loosened your grasp, it would be difficult if not impossible to again find the rope. You could freeze to death.

The horses had to be "sharp shod" in the wintertime in order to be able to walk on ice. They would leave the road and get on the river of their own accord, because the frozen roadbed would hurt the "frogs" of their feet, whereas they could walk on the ice with the sharp shoes digging in with each step.

We fought our battles with nature, and accepted them as readily as the changing of the seasons. I rode ten miles each way to school on one of the two saddle horses that I had, rotating the horses. I rode when the snow on the ground was deep enough to drag my feet in the stirrups. It was as deep as the horse's belly.

In the summers, I worked in the hayfields, starting the year after I hired out on a ranch inside the Rosebud Indian Reservation. The reservation was forty to fifty miles square and my job was twofold. I broke wild horses straight from the range, that had never felt a rope on their necks. We would segregate the stallions from the mares and break them for saddle horses. If they didn't buck — if they just crouched — we would break them to the harness and sell them for team horses.

The life was rustic and stark, but I never thought of it as being dangerous or even out of the ordinary. It was the work ranch hands did, and still do seventy years later, in places where machines haven't completely taken over.

We milked wild cows, the ones without calves, so that their bags wouldn't cake up. We had three locations, with pools of water, which were designated as Lone Tree 1, Lone Tree 2 and Lone Tree 3. I would report back to the reservation where the cows were and the men would go out and pick up the mother cow, put her in a pen and milk her right on the ground until she went dry. Very often, because of the lack of attention, and milking, the cow's bag (which is made up of four sections) would be already caked or clogged. In order to open up the milk ducts, we ran a silver needle up into the teat and try to get the milk to drain.

Often, we could save all or part of the bag, though her capacity to produce milk might be reduced by a fourth or so.

One summer South Dakota suffered a withering drought. There was a collective group of cattlemen, who got together over the years and drove their cattle to Montana, where the water and grass was. That year you could trace the trail they took by the carcasses on the road.

Every day I woke up to something new. I ate beef jerky for the first time, served to us by the wife of the man who owned the ranch where I worked. Regardless of the weather, she would slaughter young calves and preserve the meat in jars.

In South Dakota, there were lake beds as a result of rainwater that would not drain off. The lake beds would be anywhere from a few inches to a few feet deep, and would cover eight, ten or twelve sections of land. Sometimes, big haystacks would get caught up in them and be surrounded by water. Ducks and geese would stay on the lakes at night, and forage during the day in the cornfields. If you could get close enough, you could pick off the ducks because they would be flying low in order to land on the water. Kneeling on a raft with my shotgun, I was able to shoot the geese and float out to get them.

The state legislature appropriated $25,000 to bring pheasants into the state. You couldn't hunt them for several years and they were so tame you could almost feed them out of your hand. When the season opened, you could only kill one cock (it was against the law to shoot the hens) per year, and now pheasant hunting is one of the great industries in South Dakota.

In this respect, it was a storybook way for a boy growing into manhood, a rustic and pastoral life. Now and again, my mother and stepfather would go onto the reservation and drive for a number of miles to camp on the Missouri River. They fished for a day or so and then came back. We owned a few head of cattle and somewhere along the line I acquired a dog that was half collie and half coyote, named Skipper. We trained the dog to stop all cattle and horses from leaving through an open gate, and to help us cut out the cattle if that needed to be done. Frequently, when I got up in the morning Skipper would be playing with the coyotes, but when I called he came instantly, his ears erect. I raised him from the time he was a puppy, until after I went to live in town and go to high school.

One day, he got into a fight with a pit bull and was badly beaten. He dragged himself home and I made him a place by the fire and treated his wounds until he recovered. Months later, I passed the man on the street, walking with the pit bull that had injured my dog. He bred them, and reveled in their ability to fight.

He turned his dog loose, and he clamped onto my dog's hip. Then Skipper got a leg, flipped him, caught him by the throat and chewed until blood poured. The man told me to call off my dog and I said, "The hell I will. You wouldn't call off your dog when he was getting the best of mine. Now we'll let them fight." Skipper chewed until he ripped out the soft part of the pit bull's throat. Then he grabbed his jaw and pulled his jaw completely off. We left the pit bull dead in the street.

I know this story will cause revulsion in people, especially women, dogs killing dogs. But it happened, and it was a fair fight.

I kept Skipper outside my apartment over a print shop, and he slept on a pallet outside the front door. One day he turned up missing. Now, this was a very small town and there were not many places he could have gone. Finally, someone told me he was out at so-and-so's ranch on the outskirts of town. I went out there and, sure enough, there was my dog. He came running to me when he saw who I was. The man said he had found him running around, picked him up and took him home. He hadn't tried to steal him. He told me I was welcome to take him back. I started to leave with the dog, but Skipper kept looking back at the man. He would trot back toward the rancher and then look back at me. Finally, he just stopped. I took him back to the man and said, "This dog doesn't need to be in town. You keep him." I never saw the dog again.

An unexpected benefit of my schooling in South Dakota was my introduction to an opposing football player, who would become my friend and a legendary name in college coaching.

In anyone's life, you may encounter one person who qualifies as a genius at what they do. Frank Leahy did. His Notre Dame teams won four national titles, had six unbeaten seasons and a 39-game winning streak. Only one coach brought more glory to Notre Dame, and that was the immortal Knute Rockne, for whom Leahy played tackle in the late 1920's.

I met Frank when our schools played in the first game of the season in 1922. I will always remember that we lost, 50-0. I have a fuzzier memory of being knocked out, and coming to as they were carrying me off the field. I managed to get off the stretcher and went back in to finish the game.

I was the quarterback for Presho, tall but skinny as a rail at 125 pounds. I could pass and dropkick and called the signals, but making the team was no great achievement. There were no more than 18 players on the roster, and anyone who tried out could find a place to play.

During my high school years, I lettered in three sports, football, track and basketball. One year, either in 1924 or 1925, we played for the state basketball championship in the Corn Palace in Mitchell, South Dakota, and lost.

I was too preoccupied with ways of making money to think seriously about sports, beyond high school, but I loved the competition and especially the clash of wits. Once, we played against Mitchell on their court, and they had installed chicken wire just behind the basket. We noticed that the other team had soft-toed shoes, and they would drive to the hoop, stick a toe into this fence, grab the wire with one hand and with the other lay the ball in the basket.

Our team complained, but the official overruled us. Our coach asked for a volunteer to solve the problem and I stepped up. He told me to just follow the player who was dribbling the ball, and then to stand right under him after he shot, and when he came down to catch his butt on my shoulder. That would flop him to the floor pretty hard. I did just what the coach told me to do, three or four times, and they quit running up the chicken wire. We won the game.

Leahy lived in a town even smaller than ours, Winner, South Dakota, a fairly symbolic name for a young man who planned to make his career in coaching. Frank was the tailback, and ran for decent yardage when the center wasn't snapping the ball over his head. We all chewed tobacco in those days, and during that first game Leahy threw a plug at me, trying to distract me. At 16, he was a sturdy specimen at 160 pounds.

His father, also named Frank, was an Irish Catholic who dreamed of being a professional boxer. Instead, he supported his wife and six athletic children by running a trading post, and as a parttime lawman.

The oldest of the Leahy brothers, Gene, who went on to become a star halfback at Creighton, had played on weak teams at Winner. The school's fortunes turned around when they brought in a coach named Earl Walsh, who had been a teammate at Notre Dame of George Gipp, whose story was made into a movie starring Ronald Reagan. It was Walsh who recommended Frank to Rockne, and put him on his life's course.

Frank Leahy had jet black hair for as long as I knew him, and the eyes of a spaniel. He was an eloquent speaker, who referred to his players as "lads," and perfected the art of what the sportswriters called "poor-mouthing." Leahy was a master at praising the superior quality of his opponent and emphasizing how he feared for the health of his own sensitive lads, who more often than not would win by 50 points, five or take a few.

We stayed in touch until he went off to college, and I ran into him once or twice when he visited Houston. Frank was treated for cancer in Houston's M. D. Anderson hospital, and the disease killed him in 1973. His photo still hangs on the wall of my law offices.

I recognized in Leahy a hunger to achieve, and I felt it in myself. I wanted to learn, wanted to improve at whatever caught my interest, regardless of the hazards. The more I worked with my hands, the more I knew I needed to sharpen my mind. My senior year I won the state high school debating championship in Rapid City. I spent the night before the debate writing cue cards to myself, points I wanted to argue and counter.

Once I went out on my own, my junior year, I never had a dollar given to me by anybody. I had to earn my own money in order to eat and sleep. Sometimes I didn't make enough to do both. During one period, while I lived in town and went to school, I worked at two jobs. The first was at the Post Office. I got up at 4 A.M. to unlock the building and pick up a sack of mail. I carried the sack four or five blocks to the rail depot, then put it on the train that came through at around 5 A.M. In my other job, I was employed by the Farmers Elevator to unload all the coal that came into town during the winter.

I was only a sophomore when I asked for work, and the man who did the hiring asked me a question: "Son, do you know what demurrage is?" I had no idea.

"It's the fee you have to pay if you let the rail cars sit on the tracks too long. Do you think you could unload a coal car with a wheelbarrow and a scoop shovel?"

I told him, yes. I would have told him I could do it with a teaspoon and a thimble. He said, "I'm going to give you the job, but the first time I have to pay demurrage, I'll let you go." I went straight to the principal and told him that I had a job which would require me to be excused immediately, if I got a call from the Farmers Elevator, because I had a limited time to unload a ton of coal.

The school was always cooperative and a monitor would pull me out of class when the calls came. I would dash home, change my clothes and proceed to the Farmers Elevator. In the two years that I shoveled coal, I never had a car that had to pay demurrage. Occasionally, some of the members of the football team would show up to help me. Since I was the quarterback, they needed me at practice. Otherwise, I did it by myself.

I also hunted prairie chickens, quail and, in the wintertime, snowshoe rabbits. The prairie chickens would settle in for the night, and roost in a circle on the ground with their tails pointing in and their heads to the outside. When disturbed, they would begin to beat their wings. It was a frightening noise to hear, suddenly out of the quiet of the night. The way to shoot a prairie chicken is to wait until they quit flapping their wings in flight. While they were sailing, you led them just a little and fired. You'd get them every time.

The snowshoe rabbits have large feet that leave a

print like a snowshoe. In the winter, they are pure white and have the ability to lie perfectly still, even when you are right beside them. You were unlikely to see them at such times because they blended in with the snow, but you could look back and see their tracks. Your eyes could follow them literally to within inches of your own footprint.

The Dakotas still took pride in their image as The Badlands, where Wild Bill Hickcock and Calamity Jane once roamed. I once witnessed a ceremony at the Indian school at Fort Pierre, where the tribe demonstrated the ritual of rounding up and killing the buffalo. They would ride their horses alongside, jump on the back of the buffaloes and stab them to death. After the animals were butchered and skinned, a barbecue would be held.

These same rugged frontiersmen have clung to their spiritual heritage. For example, each year the understudies of the actors in the Passion Play in Oberammergau, Bavaria, in southern Germany, come to the Black Hills of South Dakota.

Wherever you turned, history and nature called out to us. In class one day, the teacher led us outside so we could view a mirage. From Presho, we could distinctly see the river in Fort Pierre, which was 40 miles away. The river appeared to be only 100 yards from where we were standing. This was the first time I knew what a mirage was. Frequently, we would also see evidence of the Northern Lights.

In another class, I heard my first radio broadcast. We had heard or read about it, but the teacher sent off for instructions on how to assemble a radio. One of my duties was to wrap foil over a carton that was about four inches in diameter; each student had something to do and then we all eagerly awaited the results. The first radio response we got was from some place in the south, where they had a dance band that played in a restaurant. We tuned in and sat there, awestruck, trying to figure out how the sound came through the air and out of the box.

And away from school, I learned about practical matters, without which real growth isn't possible. When I was 17 and living above the print shop, I ran a poker game. Well, I didn't exactly run it. Some of the local gamblers were having a hard time finding a place to play, and they asked if I would let them use my apartment. I would come in after work and go to bed while they gambled. In the morning, when I got up, my share of the pot would be left on the table for me. That may have been the easiest money I ever earned.

Although it was illegal, I also bootlegged for a short time. The dealers sometimes hired a high school kid to transport their booze. They would lend you a car, pack the back seat with whisky, and tell you to drive it to a club with a peephole on the door. The door swung open on a new hydraulic principle based on the words, "Sid sent me." You'd unload the liquor and collect the money. I would sell a bottle or two and on occasion take one with me to drink.

I don't want to be unclear about this. Alcohol has caused a good deal of trouble in this country, and others. But we botched it badly during Prohibition, when reformers denounced drinking as unhealthy, un-Christian and un-American. Human experience has shown that if it is un-anything, it is unavoidable.

At any rate, Presho, South Dakota, was not to be confused with Chicago. There would be an occasional raid, and those who were caught got a lecture and perhaps a fine. But if anything was spilled, it was bourbon or beer, not blood.

Of course, I have found over the years that it is much easier to be virtuous and righteous when you are neither poor nor hungry. There was one other boy in my class who may have been poorer than I was. He had only one parent, as I recall. On graduation day, all the boys were expected to wear a suit and necktie. I had put my money aside and bought the first suit I ever owned.

Then my friend mentioned that he was not planning to go to the graduation exercises because he didn't want to be the only boy there without a suit. I told him that although I now had one, I wouldn't wear it and we could go together, which we did.

As it turned out, the principal threatened to keep me from graduating, after I complained that the flag was not being raised and lowered properly. The principal was German, but had been in this country for many years. His objection was not on patriotic grounds, but on having his authority questioned. He called me into his office and scolded me for reporting the incident. He reminded me that I was in one of his classes. "If I decide not to pass you," he said, "you won't graduate."

I was stunned, but defiant. "You mean," I said, "that you would fail me, not because of my grades, but because I reported the manner in which you handled the flag?"

He said, "Yes, I would."

With that, I walked over to his file cabinet and pulled out my folder. It showed that if I passed my other courses that semester, I would have 19 and a half credits. I only needed 16 to graduate. It was inconsequential to me whether he gave me the grade I deserved or not.

In truth, I must have been a hard kid to evaluate, half innocent and half rebel. When I wasn't in school, or at work, I was at the pool hall, one of the few recreations I found time to enjoy.

I walked into the pool hall one day during the winter and only one man was playing. I later learned that he was a former German general who had immigrated to America, became a citizen and bought a farm near Presho. It was his custom to move into town and stay, after all the crops had been harvested. One of his great passions was billiards and he was an excellent player.

On this occasion, he asked me if I played billiards. I told him, no, that my game was pool. He then told me to get a cue and he began to explain the game to me. This casual encounter caused him to teach me some of the fine arts of billiards. He taught me how to use travel English and draw English, and it was not long before I was able to play for the house. Playing for the house meant that if I lost a game, I would not have to pay. This experience served me well when I graduated from high school in May, of 1925, and left South Dakota to return to Oklahoma.

Looking back over my life, I feel that in some ways I have been playing for the house ever since.

Section II

Clearing The Bar
May 1925 to July 1937

Chapter 2

Gone to Texas

I PICKED AN IN-BETWEEN time to graduate from high school. We did not yet realize how deeply the country was sliding into a depression. The Great War was behind us, but another would not be long in coming.

In 1925, in the White House, Calvin Coolidge was trying to set an example by his own acts of thrift. Among other economies, he reduced his budget by eliminating the gift of free pencils to newspaper correspondents, and by cutting in half the number of towels placed daily in the White House lavatories.

There were two great legal confrontations. The War Department court-martialed General Billy Mitchell, for criticizing his superiors. Mitchell was an outspoken advocate for an air force separate from the Army and Navy, and had caused grave consternation with his prediction that we lacked the air power to defend our Pacific islands, and it was there that the next war would likely begin.

Mitchell was a prophet, but to most military experts such talk was on a level with science fiction. They could not imagine, in 1925, how a foreign power could attack the United States across either ocean.

In Dayton, Tennessee, two towering legal performers — Clarence Darrow and William Jennings Bryan — matched their eloquence in the Scopes "Monkey Trial," in a duel over the Tennessee law that banned the teaching of evolution.

Among other major news events, Miriam (Ma) Ferguson was sworn in as governor of Texas, an office her husband had held ten years earlier and lost through impeachment. After repeating the oath of office, she kissed a small, worn Bible, the same one Sam Houston had kissed in 1859.

I had no way of knowing then that I would become more than casually interested in the law, and in Texas politics.

I was going through the push-pull of anyone who had been able to finish high school in those days. The Twenties were in full swing, but they were not exactly roaring in South Dakota.

My stepfather had bought an old jalopy, a Chevrolet coupe, and we started out to drive from Presho to Blackwell, Oklahoma, where my mother had gone ahead of us some months earlier. The trip was uneventful, with one exception. I fell asleep at the wheel and the car went off the road and into a deep ditch. Luckily, the ditch was dry and the mishap did no major damage to the car, or to us. I was able to get back on the road and we completed the trip.

This was not a time in America when you had choices. I had college in the back of my mind, but first there was the more practical matter of finding work. I lived with my mother and stepfather, and I needed to pay my way.

Jobs were scarce in Blackwell. I knocked on doors for weeks, until I finally landed a job in a clothing store that was "going out of business." You have seen such stores in New York, and you figure they must be franchised. Their sign stays up for years, and the customers keep coming to take advantage of the bargains.

So every night the trucks would deliver a shipment of new merchandise to the store. I was not born to sell, but with any job I ever had I poured myself into it. I worked on commission and, on one occasion, I was helping a woman who had her eye on a large amount of material. The store owner sensed this and artfully tried to lure the customer away to avoid paying my commission. I called him to one side and told him this was my customer, and I intended to earn the commission. I appreciated his help, I said, and if we teamed up perhaps we could make an even bigger sale. Which we did. Even then, I found I had an instinct for heading off a disagreement, or turning it in my favor. But, finally, the store did close its doors and I was looking for another job.

I landed one in a textile plant, and was assigned to what was called the "kill room." The air was so filled with floating particles that you could not see more than a few feet in front of you. There was no such thing as safety regulations, and no one knew or thought much about toxins and lung disease. You heard a constant chorus of coughing in that room, from breathing in those particles. During our lunch break, a worker who was middle aged, and looked older, sat next to me. He said, if I knew what was good for me I'd quit before I ruined my health. So I left the second day, which is probably my record for holding a job the shortest length of time.

I am grateful for that kindly advice. He had been there for years and had resigned himself to his fate. But he warned me that if I stayed, I would have trouble the rest of my life.

If you really want to work, you might not find a job but you can always find out where to look. The word spreads among the down and out. I heard they were hiring in the oil fields. At a corner on Main Street, men with experience on oil rigs would sit or stand at the curb each morning at six, and see if someone would hire them. This was the procedure: a truck would stop and the driver would say he was looking for two men for this, two for that and, say, eight for a four-inch pipe screw connection gang. That meant four who carried the tongs, one to thread the collar, one stabber, one on the jackboard and one jackman. It was a whole new language.

When there was any announcement by one of the trucks, men would scramble to fill up the back. If they had more than was needed, the ones with their legs hanging over the side were asked to get off. I had no oil field experience, but I watched this ritual for a week or so, and made up my mind to try my luck the next time they called for a pipe connection gang.

I didn't have to wait long. I jumped into the middle of the truck and sat down. The driver took us to an oil field and turned us over to the foreman, a man named Jap Menace (which sounds like a patriotic comic strip character during World War II.) He looked over the day workers, spotted my pale face — the others were tanned — and asked me if I had ever worked in the fields.

Sure, I lied, and I was pale because I had been working more recently inside a store. He was clearly skeptical, and pointed in the general direction of one of the oiler tanks about a half block away. "Go over there," he said, "and get the jackboard and bring it to me." I didn't have a clue as to what I was looking for, but I knew the direction.

Fortunately, there was a man painting the sides of the tanks, so I asked him if he had seen a jackboard. He pointed it out and I picked up the jackboard and brought it to Jap.

When we moved the first joint, it was obvious I didn't know what I was doing. Jap shouted at me, "If you can't work the damned jackboard then just hold the pipe," which I did. The jackman was friendly to me and by the time we engaged three or four joints, he had explained the process to me. After that I performed my task in an acceptable manner.

I watched what everyone did, and had an almost obsessive interest in the action. Laying pipe was hard labor, meant for men who were strong or desperate. I worked seven days a week, starting at seven o'clock. We were paid for ten hours; the nine we worked and a half-hour each way for ride time — to the fields and back. In the next eighteen months I worked at nearly all of the different jobs, including the collar pounder, jackman and even the stabber, the prince of the crew. I spent one week on a Mahoney pipe machine, which automatically screwed the pipe in place. We had different assignments to get the pipe up and feed it into the machine, and so far as I know they were never too successful in the oil fields.

Finally, the day arrived when Jap announced to everybody that all the work was caught up. He thanked the men for their efforts. Then he told me that Mr. Reese E. McGee wanted to talk to me the next morning at Mr. McGee's home in Blackwell. I knew where it was, so I walked over to Mr. McGee's house and they offered me a job.

I can't say for certain what caught their eye. But I was probably the only person in the whole gang with a high school education, besides Jap Menace. They knew I was young and wanted to finish my education. I worked for him for the better part of a year.

Reese E. McGee was a pipeline contractor, one of the busiest in all of Oklahoma. He said he had a job for me in Ponca City. I was to load a truck with all the equipment necessary to take up a mile of four-inch screw pipe out of the ground. In Ponca City I was to find a place to stay, then take the truck to the pool halls, hire a crew, go to the Marland tank farm and remove the pipe. I was in the same position Jap Menace

38

held when he hired me. (E. W. Marland, a prominent oil producer, later became governor of Oklahoma.) After I had the gang going, I phoned Blackwell and gave them the names of the men. McGee made out the checks and sent them to me to distribute to the men.

When the job was completed, I let everybody go. I cleaned up the tools and then the truck driver and I drove back to Blackwell and went in to see Jap Menace. He paid me a fine compliment. He said if I ever needed a job and he had one available, I would get it. He had taken a liking to me; I was stubborn and a good worker.

Those jobs on the pipeline, toiling under a relentless Oklahoma sun, helped convince me I needed to go to college. I thought I had saved enough money, and I told my mother and my stepfather that I was going to Norman to enroll at the University of Oklahoma. I registered for classes and then discovered, to my surprise, that no jobs were available. It never occurred to me to find one before I enrolled.

I had a talent for finding work, but now I learned that all the jobs were snapped up by the students who had been there the previous year. I even offered to work in the insane asylum on the opposite side of the city from the college, but they had no openings.

Feeling forlorn and, for one of the few times in my young life, rejected, I returned to Blackwell and broke the news to my mother. It was at this point that she offered a suggestion that required my swallowing some pride. She said she would call my father in Houston and perhaps he could help me get into a school there. As a result of that call, I left Blackwell and moved in with my father, and his second wife and their child, in Houston, at 2020 Oxford Street in the Heights. The year was 1927.

He had not been a presence in my life, and our relationship never developed into anything resembling closeness or affection. He had deserted us when I was a baby, and he could regain neither my respect nor my love. I had a rough and at times rootless childhood, but his absence was not my motivation to succeed, nor did I have a need to make him feel guilty. In spite of the gulf between us, I knew he would have helped me, if he could.

My father was a carpenter and a steeple jack, who worked out of the Purdy Lumber Yard at 420 Yale Street. I assisted him on one or two smokestack jobs. As I usually did, I learned on the job. In order to paint a smokestack, the painter would pull his rigging to the top of the stack, then get out of the harness. Having guided the rope, he would move himself and the rig, one hand at a time, to where he could paint another strip down the pipe. As you raised it off the ground to a sufficient height, you would keep the buckets of paint and brushes on the seat, and paint a swath about two or three feet wide from top to bottom.

Early on, I learned that every job had its mysteries, its skill and challenge. Each one was a step, some trickier than others, on the ladder that led to my becoming a lawyer. I respected them all.

I worked with my father for a short period of time, learning how to paint and helping him to build houses. We built several that are still standing in the Heights today, over sixty years later. I had gotten professional enough that I could paint the outside of a one-bedroom house with one coat, in a day. I could do the same on the inside — one coat, one day.

Friction developed almost immediately with my father's wife, and after they moved to 25th Street in the Heights the living arrangement reached a point where it was uncomfortable for me. By then I had spent a year in law school, at night, and was the only person in the class who did not have a college degree. I explained to my father, who was uneducated, that I had to get more education before I could complete law school, and this would interfere with my working because I could not get the credits I needed at night.

Our parting was without emotion, a bit awkward for my father, a relief to his wife and to me. I then went to the lumber company and talked to the owners, Mrs. Purdy and her son, Jackson, who was an aspiring playboy and owned a Chrysler. I asked Mrs. Purdy if I could work for her during the hours I was not in school. She said, yes, they could use me to assist in getting the plans and specifications for the houses.

I thanked her for the job and asked if I could build a bedroom in the rear of the lumber yard. She consented. It wasn't fancy, but I had a shower, a place to shave, sleep and hang my clothes, which were few.

In those days, the lumber yard was the contractor and would sell houses directly to the buyers. Using various books of model plans, we would discuss with the customer what he or she wanted, and what it would cost as a turnkey job. Then we drew the plans and issued the work order for the house, employed the carpenters, plumber, electrician and others who did the construction. We collected from the customer or, in some cases, from the bank.

Everything was standard, so you knew how long it would take to build. I could take a house with two bedrooms, living, dining and a bathroom, with a one or two-car garage, and figure almost to the penny how much the material and supplies would cost, down to the lumber, paint and nails.

I spent about nine months living at the Purdy Lumber Company, during which time I collected the monthly notes, including payments from blacks who worked as waiters in the railroad dining cars and could afford to buy a house. As time passed, my responsibilities grew.

The man in charge of the yard was stealing from Mrs. Purdy, and when I reported it to her she fired him. In effect, I took over some of his duties. She and her son, Jackson, were always in need of money. What I collected was usually in cash, sometimes a check, and I would place it in the cash register. Trips to the bank were few, because she or Jackson or both kept the register empty most of the time. She would come to me frequently and say she needed money right away. I soon learned to keep uncollected some of the notes that were due us. So when Mrs. Purdy needed cash, I would borrow Jackson's car and collect on the payments I had put aside. She thought I was a wizard at being able to produce money when she really needed it.

The Purdys lived across a bayou from the lumber yard, and I helped build a bridge across the bayou. Meanwhile, I had registered at Rice Institute in September, of 1927. The school, endowed by a reclusive millionaire named William Marsh Rice, had a small private enrollment and had just graduated its 10th class a year earlier.

The distance from Yale Street to the Rice campus, through downtown to South Main, was about six miles. I had to hitch hike both ways for my classes, which began at 8 A.M., and I never missed an 8 o'clock class in three years. You made the trip in two legs. It was fairly easy to get a ride downtown. And it became a custom for a Rice student to stand on the corner of Main and McKinney, and someone would always come along to take you out there.

I met Frank Mandell, who was a year ahead of me at Rice, and we went in together to rent a large apartment at 902 Bartell. We sublet two rooms to two men who were selling advertisements in the telephone book. They worked for a man in Kansas City, who had a contract with the phone company. They were paid on a commission basis, but they made more money than I had ever seen for so little work.

Eventually, when the contract ran out, the telephone company refused to renew the man's contract and established their own, now familiar Yellow Pages. I have sometimes wondered if the man had hired a good attorney, he might have drawn a contract differently so as to protect his interests. He might still own the Yellow Pages today. One of the men who sold the ads later married a young girl from Galveston, and from time to time over the years I would see them when I visited the island.

Frank was a rather short, slight young man, apparently brilliant, but with certain qualities I disliked as I came to know him better. In short, he was somewhat dishonest. He was printing the *DeMolay Magazine* for the Masonic Lodge, and selling advertising to support it. I accidentally opened a closet one day and it was stacked almost to the ceiling with magazines. He had not distributed any copies, except to the advertisers, and was printing far less than he had represented.

Frank was a hustler. When Epsom Downs was open, and the horses were running, he published a tip sheet and made money faster than he could count it — as much as a thousand dollars a day. This was when a job on an oil rig might pay eighty dollars a month. Then Frank would wind up betting against his own tip sheet and blowing it all.

I'm not sure how much of this we can attribute to the decade of the Twenties, what Paul Gallico called The Age of Wonderful Nonsense. That year, 1927, Charles Lindbergh made his heroic solo flight across the Atlantic to Paris. U.S. Marines landed in Nicaragua to protect American mining interests during a period of political "unrest." Two anarchists, named Sacco and Vanzetti, were executed in Massachusetts for murders they may not have committed. Gene Tunney defended his heavyweight title, defeating Jack Dempsey in the fight that became famous for the referee's "long count." Babe Ruth broke his own

44

home run record, hitting 60 for the New York Yankees.

The next year, Houston would be the host city for the Democratic national convention, where Al Smith, the governor of New York and a Catholic, would be nominated as his party's presidential candidate. (He would lose to Herbert Hoover.) And in 1929, a decade that began with a bang, and prohibition, would end with a high, shrill whimper. October 29, 1929 was Black Friday, the day the bottom fell out of the stock market.

I had attended Rice for two and a half years, before having to withdraw because I came down with mumps in the latter part of my junior year. I was still determined, still shooting for that degree, but I needed to regroup, and find some way to keep the moths from eating my billfold.

While I was at Rice, and living at 902 Bartell, I met one of the most intriguing characters I have ever known — Roy Hofheinz. He was a freshman my sophomore year, and he used our apartment as a hangout. He drove an orchid-colored Ford, with side curtains that were not waterproof. He frequently brought girls to the apartment and embarrassed them beyond my wildest imagination by telling stories about their shared experiences.

In general, he was a pretty obnoxious individual, an impression Roy did not outgrow in the minds of many, who dealt with him when he was the most controversial mayor the city ever had, and later as the creator of the Astrodome, the world's first covered sports stadium.

He was a boy wonder politician, Lyndon Johnson's first campaign manager, and the youngest county judge, at 24, ever to hold that office in the nation's history. He made his money in radio and real estate, and at one time owned an interest in the Barnum and Bailey Circus — the almost perfect pairing.

I believe Roy busted out of Rice after his freshman year. One experience may illustrate what I regarded as his brassiness. There was a party one night in the apartment, and someone discovered a young man who was so drunk he had no recollection of his name or where he lived. Roy's solution was to call the police and a newspaper reporter.

I felt sorry for the fellow and provided a quiet space where he could sleep it off. Then I checked his wallet and found a note with a room number at the Plaza Hotel, which I called. His father answered the phone, and before I could tell him the circumstances he barked: "What kind of trouble is he in now?"

I said, none, but for the moment he was unable to take care of himself. His father made it clear he didn't want him around. I let him stay for a week to ten days, but had to keep hiding the liquor from him. He had a talent for finding it. After he sobered up, he told us he had been to a party in the building and started back to his father's apartment at The Plaza, but became disoriented.

We said our good-byes and wished him luck, and sometime later I read in the paper that he was killed somewhere in West Texas in an automobile accident.

One of my odd jobs was working at the Bon Ton

Cleaning and Pressing establishment at Main and McKinney. I went to my classes at Rice in the mornings, and with the exception of one day a week, when I had a lab in the afternoon, I would get to my job around one o'clock and work until they closed around eleven at night. On week ends, I worked from the time they opened in the morning until closing. We did cleaning, pressing, shoe shines and laundry service.

I may have lacked polish, and I certainly lacked funds, but no one could accuse me of lacking initiative. I made a deal with the laundry to offer Rice students a two-for-one special: two suits cleaned and pressed for one dollar. I picked up the suits, took them to the cleaning wagon and then returned them, keeping part of the dollar as my fee. That plan was so good it lasted only a couple of weeks. The Rice athletic department put me out of business, informing me that the concession had been give to Claude Bracey, a sprinter on the track team.

The Bon Ton was next door to "One's-a-Meal," a Houston diner where the service was quick and the food portions were ample.

I got to know the owner of One's-a-Meal. He would come into the restaurant dressed like a laborer, look around, then go in the back and tell the manager what could be corrected or improved. I believe he had the first concept of fast food. They had several waiters and waitresses, but only one man to do the cooking. The cook had trained himself to remember the orders in perfect sequence when they came in.

While I was present one day, the owner was discussing a new item on the menu, a fruit plate, and told

47

his employees not to push it too hard because he didn't make as much profit on that particular order as he did others. At that time, you could get two scrambled eggs, three pieces of raisin toast and coffee for a quarter. Bacon or sausage cost ten cents extra.

There was a chain of sandwich shops headquartered in either New York or Chicago who tried to hire the cook away. Although they offered him a higher salary, he said he would rather stay in Houston. At its peak in the late 1950's, One's-a-Meal had outlets all over the city. I think two are still in operation today, one on Memorial Drive and another on West Gray.

It would not have been possible to draw a chart of their clientele. A few booths apart, you would see a skid row bum drinking coffee, and couples in formal clothes who had dropped by after a wedding or a prom. They were among the few places in Houston that stayed open all night.

During my tenure at Rice, I got involved in promoting dances in order to support myself and pay tuition. We had scheduled a dance at the River Oaks Country Club, featuring Lee's Owls, composed of musicians from the school band and an orchestra that performed on the roof of the Rice Hotel. This was during my illness, in my junior year, and I wrote an ad and asked Frank Mandell to take the copy over to *The Thresher*, the campus newspaper, and ask if they would run the ad across the bottom of the front page. We called the dance the "Collegiate Wingding."

Frank took it upon himself to rewrite the ad, a development I learned about when I got a call from

Rice officials. They said the ad was incorrect, and if I didn't call off the dance I would be expelled. It seems Frank had inserted the word "ex-officio" in the text, which meant "on official permission by Rice." Although guests were already arriving at the dance, I had no option but to cancel it. I paid whatever money I could to the orchestra and later made up the remaining payments to them. I sent a friend out to River Oaks Country Club, and they said they counted some seventy-plus automobiles already parked or heading into the driveway, at the appointed time of the dance. That setback did nothing to restore my health and less for my bank balance.

But we kept trying. Louis Rosenberg, who is now dead, and I put on some dances, one of which was at the end of Main Street in a large dance hall. We had booked the two orchestras, and I was selling the tickets and Louis received them as the people came through the door. When we reached the break even point, I turned that ticket edgewise in the box. Then I walked up to Louis and told him this ticket amounted to our breaking even; the rest of it was gravy.

During this same time frame, Roy Hofheinz staged dances in another part of the city called "Yo Yo" dances. You had to have a yo yo in order to get inside. If you didn't have a yo yo, you couldn't get into the dance even if you bought a ticket.

Every year was a new struggle to stay in school. At one point, I went to see the bursar at Rice, a Mr. McCants, and told him I needed to borrow money for my expenses. He said I didn't qualify for a student loan, but he would make an exception in my case. The school had a student loan fund at the old Union National Bank at Main and Congress, where I was able to borrow around $300. After leaving school and finding a job, I was able to go to the bank and pay off my debt. The bank officer told me that I was one of the very few students to pay off a school loan.

But even that incident had a twist. I did a joint venture with a friend, Jack Reeves, in hopes of generating a few dollars to apply toward my schooling. When we learned that the Democratic convention was coming to Houston, Jack and I went to the city and leased the vacant lot across the street from where City Hall now stands. When the city realized that the convention people would need that lot for parking, they notified us that our lease had been canceled. Jack and I subsequently sued the city and the case was settled. I was working in Louisiana, in the oil fields, when the settlement came through, and that was the money I used to pay off my student loan at the Union National Bank.

One way or another, I was learning about the law. I was also learning about how to handle money, which may or may not be connected. I was still in school, and driving a Dodge I had bought in Chicago for $25, when the Barrett Company called and asked if I could inspect their paint, which was being applied to a short job in Oxford, Mississippi. I agreed, drove to Oxford and checked into the hotel where the crew was staying. I picked the key people and took them to dinner.

I noticed that many of the people in the dining room were eating quail, so I asked the manager where they bought them. He pointed to a black man, a porter, and said, "He'll put all the quail you want in a box for 25 cents a bird, and he furnishes his own ammunition." I figured up how many I needed to feed the people on my crew, and he dropped the quail in a box and I had them cooked for that evening's meal.

The man in charge of the construction gang was someone I knew, and he had a large reputation for drinking and fighting. The story was told that he would get drunk and then, standing in his hotel room, he would kick the top of the door frame and sometimes the ceiling. But he always paid for the damages.

He did not come down for dinner that night, so we ate and I put some quail aside for him. I finished my plate, excused myself, picked up the container of quail I had put aside and asked for his room. The desk clerk advised me not to disturb him; the last fellow who went up there had been thrown down the stairs. I went up anyway. He and another man were sitting on the floor, flat on their butts, sharing a bottle. He recognized me and I handed him the container. He opened it up, and ate the quail, bones and all, and told me that was the best "pork chop" dinner he had ever eaten in his life. He was so drunk he thought the quail were pork chops.

When I left Rice, I couldn't find a satisfactory job. I met and worked for Ash Robinson, who was then selling Southern Thrift (an insurance program for workers) at Texas Gulf Sulphur Company in New Gulf, Texas. I was living in a boarding house in New Gulf and, although I had sold some Southern Thrift policies to some of the workmen and sent in the paperwork, along with the money, I did not get any replies from Ash nor any commission. It therefore became necessary for me to go to Houston to see what was wrong.

I left New Gulf with just the clothes on my back, and when I contacted Ash he told me the company had folded and he did not have any money to pay me. I was totally without funds. When I called my landlady to tell her I would pay her as soon as I was able, she told me she had already sold my belongings to settle the bills.

Ash Robinson later made a fortune in oil, but he is perhaps better remembered in Houston, and elsewhere, for the mysterious death of his daughter, Joan. When Joan's husband, Dr. John Hill, who had been accused of causing her death, was murdered in a professional hit, many amateur crime fans suspected that Ash had brought in his own verdict. The case became the subject of a best-selling book, *Blood and Money.*

I took a job in Houston selling retail ads on commission, which meant that you did not get paid until you made the sale. There followed a period of about three and a half days when I had no money for food and no place to sleep. While working at the Bon Ton I had established credit, and they carried me during this time, enabling me to get a shoe shine, a freshly pressed suit and clean laundry. The engineer in the building across the street was a friend of mine, and he permitted me to stop in and shave and take a bath. Every day I would go out on the street looking flush, hungry as hell and trying to hustle a sale.

For those three or four days, without food or lodging, I would stand in front of the Bon Ton when the *Houston Post* would be delivered and wait for a few copies to be dropped in the trash can. I collected three or four papers and would walk to the graveyard near City Hall, loosen my tie and belt, take off my shoes, spread the papers on the grass, lie down on them and catch a couple of hours of sleep. The reason I selected the graveyard was because I did not anticipate that any police would wander in there and arrest me for vagrancy.

I remember walking by James' Coney Island and not having a nickel to buy a hot dog. Finally, I made a $200 sale and received a commission of fifty dollars. Half-dizzy with hunger, I then made a terrible mistake. I went down to Kelly's restaurant, across the street from the Rice Hotel, ate a massive amount of food and almost died.

This scene was hardly uncommon. The cold, clammy grip of The Great Depression was everywhere, with its bread lines and boxcar migrants and brother-can-you-spare-a-dime desperation.

In 1930, when I had to drop out of Rice, I found out Frank Mandell had been taking money from me and the other men who were living in the building. (Since he was older than I, our apartment was in Frank's name and he handled all the cash transactions.) He had not been paying the bills, in particular the one from Jett's Grocery. The store advised me, while I was ill in bed, that we owed more than $400, a helluva lot of money at that time. Frank began to tell me that I had to help him pay the bill. I told him I had nothing in my pocket but lint. He had mismanaged the money and it was his problem. I just walked out of the apartment. Frank was a brilliant young man, but he had a flawed character.

Finally, I was offered an attractive job with United Gas if I agreed to go to San Antonio, where they were building a pipeline in the area around San Marcos and New Braunfels. I was broke, but I hitch-hiked to San Antonio, slept in the lobby of the Gunter Hotel and reported for work at the proper time as a paint inspector for the pipeline. I lived in a boarding house not far from the St. Anthony Hotel, and worked there for several months. I got my first intro-duction to Barrett pipeline enamel, the paint we were applying to the pipe.

When the job was finished, Mr. Nickels, whose nickname was "Thunderbolt," told me there was an-other pipeline laying job in Lake Charles and that I could go there as a paint inspector if I was willing. I told him, yes. I became casual friends with a man named Lance, who was a welding inspector on the same job, and we drove to Lake Charles in the 1925 Dodge he and his wife owned.

The Louisiana job involved laying fourteen-inch pipe for gas transportation. The joints were twenty feet long, with a bell at one end. The two bells were welded together and the other end had a Dresser coupling on it. Because of the weather conditions, and the condition of the ditch in which the pipeline was being laid — some of the lowlands were flooded — we were up to our knees in water all day long. The walls of the ditch would crumble and would have to be cleaned out.

We were unable to lay much of any line, and because the condition of the paint and wrapping being put on the pipe were not satisfactory to me, I shut the job down. The wrapping machine would not adjust to the difference in the size of the pipe, and was not adhering to it. This would be a source of future trouble down the line.

The superintendent of construction came out and said if I did not let them do it the way they wanted to do it, he would call United Gas and I would probably get fired. Given the times, and the scarcity of jobs, this was no snap judgment. But I told him to go ahead. It was two or three days before anyone showed up, and it was Thunderbolt.

In the interim, I had asked the workmen to cut the wrapping with a knife and when it reached the bell it had to be hand turned. The joint was wrapped with an Osenberger wrapper, which I obtained on loan from a man who sold wrappings, in the hope that he would be able to make a sale.

When Mr. Nickels showed up, we went out to the job. I told the superintendent to demonstrate what he wanted to do. He painted the joint the way he wanted. The next joint I painted the way I wanted. Nickels turned to the superintendent and said, "Fred is doing the job I hired him to do. Whatever he says goes, so if you want to finish the job do what he says."

He invited me to have a drink with him and then he left for Houston. As a result of this encounter, the superintendent was not very happy, so in a few days one of the men who was engaged in melting the coal tar pitch enamel that was a coating for the pipe, said: "Fred, the superintendent has hired a professional prize fighter to run you off the job." He offered to stay close to me and he assured me that when the fighter showed up he would get in no more than one punch, because he (my new friend) was carrying a 32-inch Stilton wrench and he wasn't reluctant to use it. The fighter did appear, and he walked up to me and asked if I knew who he was and what he had been hired to do.

I told him he might whip the hell out of me that day, but he would have to do it every day. And I didn't know if he sensed the presence of the man with the wrench at my side, but whatever the case he walked away. We had no more trouble except for one other incident.

A relative of one of the higher ups had been sent down and given a job, even though no jobs were available. My inspector said I was to look after him. Several days went by and one day I received a call telling me he was in jail. I went down to the station and asked what charges were filed against him. The desk sergeant said, "Fishing."

I was dumbfounded, momentarily. I said, it isn't against the law to fish.

He said, "It is if you are fishing with dynamite." The relative had found some dynamite and would throw the sticks into the pond and sweep up the fish when they floated to the surface. I reported what had happened, knowing the inspector couldn't fire him.

Later, he made an even more costly mistake. This one forced us to replace some pipe and when I again recommended his firing, the company got rid of him. The wheels of justice often turn slowly, but at least they do turn.

BIG SKY, BIG SHOULDERS

As the Louisiana work neared completion, Thunderbolt told me, as well as another crew member, that a utility company in Montana had a project laying an 18-inch natural gas pipeline. We accepted his offer to work in the Treasure State and off we went, with his wife. The three of us slept in the car, and drove straight through the nearly 2,500-mile trip.

As I recall, we had to lay one hundred miles of pipe in forty-foot joints welded in a continuous line. It was a new, high carbon steel pipe manufactured by A. O. Smith, in Milwaukee, and shipped to the job.

We were close to the Canadian border and frequently went across to have a few beers — it was prohibition — and sometimes smuggled a few across in the car. Luck was still with me. Earl Allen was the Barrett Company service representative on the job in Montana. Earl would become a lifelong friend and a fellow Houston Club member until his death.

Earl and Bob Roberts, who had been in the Kansas City office, had discussed hiring me as a service manager when the Montana pipeline was done. I told them I would not be able to respond until I talked to Thunderbolt, who had given me jobs in Texas, Louisiana and Montana. I would stick with him if he needed me.

Thunderbolt didn't know if he would have any future work for me. He advised me to take the Barrett job and I did. Roberts told me the salary and the rules of using an expense account (the kind of indoctrination you couldn't get at the Harvard Business School). He also explained that as we traveled and serviced the different jobs, we were required to wear a uniform which consisted of boots, regular pants, jacket and special hats.

To celebrate my hiring, I joined Bob and Earl Allen for a drink, and with it came a lesson I have never forgotten. Bob had offered me $450 per month and expenses, an excellent job at that time. But after the company made it official, he told me the salary would be $500. I didn't contradict him.

Part of our equipment was a camera to take pictures and a typewriter to make daily reports. The mails were dependable in those days and we would mail the report on Saturday to 40 Rector Street in New York, with our route list and changes for the following week.

When the Montana job was completed, Bob and I went by train to Kansas City, where he lived. We picked up a Barrett car and drove to Chicago, and I was assigned a job for one of Sam Insell's pipeline companies. I worked for the Barrett Company for three years as a service manager and drove 50,000 miles a year in a Model "A" Ford, doing jobs in fourteen states, from California to New York, and parts of Canada.

I made my headquarters in Chicago living in such hotels as The Stevens, which was a great wonder to me because it had three thousand rooms with three thousand baths and was the largest hotel in the world. For a time, I lived with my mother in a house at 9500 South that I rented on a month to month basis.

When we moved to the south side of Chicago, our lives took a more interesting turn. We had been in the house for about three days when the doorball rang and a man at the door said he was in charge of the ward. He was a Democrat and said if either my mother or me needed transportation to the polls to call him. He wanted to welcome us to Chicago and noticed I had a Texas license plate on my car. He added that one of his services was taking care of speeding or parking tickets: Just bring it to him and he would take care of it. That was my introduction to politics.

While I worked in Chicago, the company laid a lot of pipe in the area and I commuted to the pipeline and home. It was during this period that the Federal Government tried Al Capone for tax evasion. I recall betting that he would be convicted, based on my one year of law school and my firm belief that I knew everything about the law. In any event, I won the bet.

Those were electrifying times. There were mob wars in Chicago, soup kitchens and street vendors selling apples. The banks closed. I had my money in Postal Savings, so it didn't affect me, but I read avidly what the newspapers were saying had caused the "Bank Holiday."

The bank for the Ford Motor Company in Detroit was the main office for a bank that had branch offices in different cities surrounding Detroit. The story went that the bank called in Mr. Ford and told him they were having a cash problem. They wanted him to know before he heard it elsewhere. They asked him to keep his money in the bank.

58

The article quoted Mr. Ford as saying: "Gentlemen, this is what I will do. You step aside and I will take the bank over because apparently you have not been able to run it with efficiency. I will guarantee all the obligations of the bank." They refused, he withdrew his funds, they closed their doors and banks all over America fell like dominoes.

For nearly all Americans, it was frightening, watching the run on the banks until they closed. Yet it was impossible to cause the banks to run out of cash. As the people took their money out, most of them turned to Postal Savings, which deposited the money right back in the bank.

There was a report in the papers that a customer of one of the large banks in Chicago had withdrawn all of his funds in the form of a cashier's check. Then he walked over to another department of the bank, converted it into gold and stored the gold in his safety deposit box at the bank. The amount of gold he had weighed one ton; at that time, gold was selling for twenty dollars an ounce.

The Barrett Company treated me well. I experienced a number of "firsts" in my life growing out of this corporate employment, including my first airplane ride. I was on a job in Lincoln, Nebraska, when I received a call advising me to report the next day to another job in upstate New York. When I answered that I certainly couldn't drive such a distance to meet the deadline, I was told to garage my company car and take a commercial flight — which I did.

I also saw New York City for the first time. I checked into the Commodore Hotel adjacent to Grand Central Station (now the Grand Hyatt) and I arrived with seven suitcases. The room clerk quoted me rates ranging from three dollars up to six dollars. "Or do you want something higher?" he asked. I told him to give me the peddler's special, which was the three-dollar room.

Around this time, 1931, the cost of everything reflected Depression conditions. Breakfast and lunch usually cost sixty-five cents a meal, and dinner was seventy-five cents. I'd leave a dime tip.

Being on an expense account introduced me to "how the other half lives." Barrett never questioned my charges, even when I reported buying a case of whiskey in half-pint bottles, which I distributed on various jobs for "good will" purposes. I learned that my boss, Bob Roberts, judged performances in part by eyeing expense accounts. He fired one man for spending too much, but another for spending too little. Roberts rightly concluded that the latter individual was not adequately covering his territory, or his responsibility. To hide the truth, he was jacking up his automobile and running the odometer with the car in place.

When working for the pipeline paint division of Barrett lagged, I was assigned to the company's roofing segment. One assignment took me to Detroit, where I was expected to interview roofing companies to determine their charges for services. The objective, in those Depression days, was to establish "fair trade" codes for industry. I was assigned the task of collecting information from our competitors.

A manager of one company resisted vigorously my attempt at "snooping." So I simply told him I would report his refusal to cooperate and he immediately produced his figures.

Finally, Barrett ran out of productive work for me and I had to leave. I understood perfectly and felt no resentment. I realized I had been one of the first hired and now one of the last to be let go. Some of the considerate ways I was treated by Bob Roberts and others at Barrett I have retained and followed in dealing with people who have worked for me. While I elected to pursue independent employment most of my life, I know how fortunate I had been to work in this corporate environment.

It was not long after leaving Barrett that I returned again to law school. But I did that only after working as a guide at the Chicago's World Fair, held in the years 1933 and 1934. It was during that experience that I first saw an operating television set, with its grainy black and white images. We had seen the future, and it was 21-inches in diameter.

At one point, my assignment was to accompany VIP's around the Fairgrounds. It was my good fortune to escort the famous Will Rogers on tour one day. No one could have been more gracious.

My law studies resumed with the fall semester of 1934 and continued into 1937. During these final law school days, as always, I worked to support myself. My tastes had improved greatly due to my employment time with the Barrett Company, but it seemed that I was still destined to meet my living needs by working at various jobs. At any rate, law school was finally a thing of the past for me and I looked forward to whatever was next.

Section III

The Mobile Lawyer December 1942 to September 1945

Chapter 3

From Bar to War

WHEN I WAS ADMITTED to the Texas State Bar on July 12, 1937, Houston was a city dominated by big money, big oil and big law. True then, true now.

Of course, all the big institutions in town were so closely knit it amounted to a form of incest. The top firms exercised discreet political power, were allied with the leading banks and hospitals and foundations.

Firms such as Vinson, Elkins, and Fulbright, Crooker, and Baker, Botts were already known nationally and would continue to prosper. But that path was not one I considered open to me. Nor was it one that tempted me. I never kidded myself. I had graduated from night law school. When it came to competing with the sons of well connected families, with their degrees from the Ivy League or the University of Texas, the odds were not in my favor.

If I had learned anything about myself, it was that I liked the challenge of being on my own. This was not a matter of vanity or pride. I had proven in dozens of jobs that I could follow orders. But I had a need to make my own way.

As happened so often, I received a helping hand at just the right time. I called on Jim Bracewell, the attorney for the Harris County Taxpayers' Association, at his office in the Sterling Building, to ask if he might have any extra space I could use to begin setting up my practice.

Jim was well known and respected, and with his sons, Fentress and Searcy, had founded a firm, Bracewell and Patterson, that would take its place among the city's elite. His sons would have fine legal careers of their own. Searcy became a Texas state senator. Fentress served for many years as the chairman of the port authority, supervising the ship channel. The digging of the deep water channel, fifty miles to the Gulf, was an engineering triumph that elevated Houston into the ranks of the country's most dynamic cities. Its motto for a time was, "The City That Can." If you were young and hard working ambitious, this was the place to be. We knew we could.

Jim Bracewell was in partnership with an attorney named Charley Spiner, who was Jewish. After we chatted a few minutes, Mr. Bracewell called in Charley and explained to him that I had just gotten my license to practice law and needed a place to hang my hat. They decided they could let me use an office every day except for the weekly meeting of the Jewish Loan Committee.

Once a week, the committee met with Charley Spiner and extended loans to those of the Jewish faith who had encountered financial problems and were unable to secure a loan from a bank. And that one day a week, I would make myself scarce and let Mr. Spiner and the committee conduct their business.

So through the kindness of Jim Bracewell and Charley Spiner, I opened my law practice, using their address and telephone number on the business cards I had printed.

One day I ran into a former schoolmate of mine, B. W. Payne, an attorney who was then working for an insurance company as an adjuster. (His father was then the chief of police in Houston and years later, when I traveled to Acapulco, wrote a letter of introduction for me to that city's police chief.)

Payne told me that the firm of Burris and Benton was looking for a young attorney. They had interviewed at least twenty candidates for the position, but had not yet made a decision. He thought if I applied, I would probably get hired. I went over for an interview and walked out with a job.

At the time, Burris and Benton split a draw of $900 a month from the firm. Fifty percent, or $450, went to Burris. Benton received thirty-five percent, and the remaining fifteen percent ($135) went to me. They did not have an office available, so I worked at a desk in their library. Having a fixed income, even a modest one, gave me some needed security while I literally learned the tricks of my trade.

I had been on the job about three weeks when I was called into the office of Mr. Burris. He and Benton said they wanted my opinion on why the firm wasn't making any money. The question startled me. I pointed out that they were attorneys with lengthy experience; why were they asking me?

Burris said they were aware that I had worked at a wide variety of jobs and he felt I had a good business sense. They really wanted my opinion. I owed them an honest answer and I gave them one. I told them what the young attorneys at the courthouse were saying about the firm of Burris and Benton: that they were afraid to try a lawsuit. Convinced that they wouldn't go to court, the insurance companies could drive down the settlement price. They thanked me. I was later called back into the office and was told that from then on, I would assist in the trial of three dockets for Burris and one for Benton (a Harvard graduate), and I was assigned all the other cases in the office myself. Thus started a series of trials.

At that time, the courts had a nine-month docket. I found myself in trial every week, sometimes more than once. When we concluded one, I would get a call for another. I was in court, it is safe to say, at least once a week for thirty-six weeks.

Burris was not accomplished as a trial attorney. He was more of a public relations type, who never met a stranger. He was a rainmaker, a man adept at bringing in new accounts.

Benton was very well educated, but had little or no trial experience. During the time I was with them, Benton and I never lost a case. Of course, many of them were settled before going to trial, but of those that went to a jury, we won them all. I used a lot of tactics that I picked up from other attorneys over the years. When I saw an attorney pull something in court that was legitimate, I didn't hesitate to copy it. If it worked for me, I made it part of my modus operandi in trying cases.

One example: If I had a difficult witness, and wanted to do the most damage to him that I could, I would finish the cross-examination and excuse him. I would wait until he got two-thirds of the way out of the courtroom and would then, say, "Your honor, I would like to have the court's indulgence and recall the witness for one or two more questions. They are important to my client." Well . . . having left the stand, thinking he had done pretty well and with his defenses down, the witness was usually apprehensive at being recalled. I would tell him he was still under oath and the penalty of perjury would apply. At that point, you could either break him, get the admission you wanted, or at the least confuse him.

When you are young, and working with a small firm that isn't deep in resources, you quickly learn to improvise. When we appealed some cases, we always filed in person, never by mail. Sometimes the briefs would not be prepared until the last day of filing, and the courthouse closed at 5:00 P.M. I had cultivated a friendship with the clerk of the court in Galveston, and would have to drive there on the week end to file the brief with the clerk at his home. He would take the brief to the courthouse on Monday and backdate the filing for me. It was a nice arrangment, but I never told Burris about it.

But this practice led indirectly to an upgrade in my lifestyle. I was on my way down to argue a case in Galveston one day and the old heap I was driving went dead. It was time to buy another car.

I knew a man who owned a car rental agency and I asked if he would look around to see if he could find a good, inexpensive car for me. He called back and said he had found one, and asked if I could wait a week or ten days. I said, yes. When the car was ready, I dropped by the agency and bought it. This is the story the dealer told me: One of the rental agencies in the east, in New York or Philadelphia, had rented the car to a man who never returned it. A warrant was put out for his arrest.

The man left a trail and was easily found. Two or three times a day, he would buy a new tire and pay for it with a cashier's check. As it turned out, he had stolen a quantity of cashier's checks in $50 and $100 amounts, and he would buy a tire for ten dollars and pocket the difference in cash. When he wasn't buying tires, he'd do the same with an oil change.

The police tracked him through the sales records and finally arrested him in Houston. The car was a brand new Chevrolet, and while it was impounded by the police the agency in the east asked my friend if he could find a buyer. He figured out what the car was worth, what it would cost to have it driven back east, and then knocked some more off the price. And that was how I happened to buy a new Chevy. I drove that car until I went into the service.

One case I tried was against a doctor, who had a

rather large interest — known only to a few people — in an insurance company. I spent a whole day poring through records in Austin and dug out the information on his interest. This insurance company hired this doctor exclusively for any workmen's compensation cases. His conflict of interest, if disclosed, posed a real danger to him. By contrast, the doctor I hired had absolutely clean hands.

I asked the other physician if he had an interest in the insurance company and he replied, no. Then I asked him if he owned any stock in the company. It must have been clear to him from my line of questioning that I had uncovered something. After an almost embarrassing pause, he said, yes, he owned stock. I then suggested to him that every time the insurance company makes a dollar, that he would benefit, for example, through dividends or a rise in the value of the stock. He said his answer would have to be yes, so he supposed that in that context he did own an interest in the company, after all.

I learned that trick from a lawyer named Henry W. Strasburqer, of Dallas.

The young attorneys of that time, and place, had a saying: if you tried a case with Strasburqer, it was like spending one year in a post-graduate law course. He would surely teach you.

Eventually, Henry and I became close friends. We tried many lawsuits as adversaries and always conducted ourselves as professionals. In the courtroom we never gave in to the other; then went out together for lunch or dinner.

Henry demonstrated many of the techniques that served me well in later years. He usually tried a case with a co-counsel, and when something really damaging to his position in the lawsuit occurred, Henry would walk out of the courtroom. He might stay out as much as thirty minutes, then return looking unconcerned. I soon discovered exactly what he was doing. During the next recess, he would have the court reporter read to him what had happened during his absence. But he had planted a notion with the jury: Mr. Strasburqer would never leave the courtroom, if anything important was being said. This ability to act unconcerned helped weaken whatever the damage had been, and he was able to bring it off because of his working knowledge of the case.

On one occasion, when Strasburqer was trying a case against a man named Frankie, who wrote a book on rules on civil procedure, I walked into the courtroom to watch. Henry came over and sat next to me. In a whisper, he asked what kind of final argument I thought the other attorney would make. I told him I had no idea, but most of his cases were criminal, so I thought he would make a logical argument on the facts.

Henry said that was the argument he could least afford. Frankie had a young lawyer as his associate, and the young man had made the opening argument. Henry's strategy was to entice the younger attorney into doing the closing argument, as well, so he started in on him, criticizing him, castigating him in every manner he could.

When Strasburqer sat down, it was the young

lawyer who rose in righteous indignation, whereupon Frankie told him to sit down, that he would reply to Henry's closing argument — that's when Frankie lost the case.

He was an unusual figure in those days, because he went wherever the action was, from El Paso to Beaumont and from north to south all over Texas. Henry was like the circuit riding preachers of days long past.

When I think back over the past 50 years, I realize how much simpler the practice of law was when I started out. Burris was friendly with a man named Earl Cox, who became a close friend of mine and eventually referred some cases to the firm on the condition that I had to try them.

Earl was a unique man with no formal education. He was a male secretary in a legal firm, who studied the law at night. He finally passed the bar and the firm he worked for hired him as an attorney, but on the stipulation that he would be his own secretary. In those days, if you wanted to be a lawyer you accepted certain inconveniences.

I once drove to Lufkin to try a case against a very savvy local attorney, J. J. Collins. On the morning of the trial, I sent my client to the courthouse and dropped by Collins' office. While we visited, I again offered a settlement, which he declined. He told me we would just have to try the case.

When we reached the courtroom, the jury was seated outside waiting to be selected. Collins proceeded to shake hands and speak to everyone of the prospective jurors on a personal basis, calling each by name. We started the trial, had a break for lunch, and returned at the appointed time. When the evening recess came at five o'clock, Collins said he wanted to see me. I told him I would meet him in his office. I told my client to go to the hotel.

Collins, a good-natured man, got right to the point. "Young man," he said, "I want to tell you something. I kinda like you. You'll make a fine lawyer one day, but you haven't got a Chinaman's chance in hell of winning this lawsuit against me here in my hometown. I have every reason to cut the amount of the settlement I offered you, but instead I'm going to increase it a little and advise you very, very sincerely to take it."

I thanked him for his candor and told him I would let him know in the morning. I went back to the hotel and talked to my client. I called Burris at home and told him the situation and that, under the circumstances, I thought we would be better off settling this case. Which we did. This particular case was my lesson in what local influences could do — the so-called home field advantage.

When you're young and everything is new, all cases seem complex and interesting. Some of them are. I took on one client who was a cleaning lady, who fainted one night while doing her job at the Humble Oil Company. Someone rushed over with a drink from a bottle and she took a swallow of it.

Immediately, she began spitting up blood and pieces of flesh. It turned out that a worker at Humble had poured a cleaning fluid for marble, which contained lye, in a water bottle and had not changed the label. This is what she had been given — ammonia.

Humble was self-insured and wouldn't offer a settlement. I sued Humble for the maximum allowed in County Court, plus her medical expenses. Humble Oil was represented by some of the top attorneys from Vinson and Elkins, but they settled the case, glad to get it behind them, and fortunate that it occurred in an era when juries were less likely to give huge awards in personal injury cases, especially to the working poor. At the end of that period, I would sue them for a like amount and would continue to do so until I had a number of suits going and some of them on appeal when they finally settled the cases.

I tried hundreds of cases in a period of about five years, and it was a very lucrative practice for three people. The income of Benton and Burris increased one hundred percent every year that I was with them.

Meanwhile, I was finding my niche. I was elected president of the Houston Junior Bar Association in 1940, and president of the Texas Junior Bar in 1942.

The only cloud over my life was the one that loomed over everyone else's: what Americans referred to with increasing frequency as the "unpleasantness" in Europe. Each passing year brought us closer to a time of great historic upheaval.

In 1939, Germany invaded Poland and as Hitler's armies menaced the rest of the continent, France and Britain declared war. It was the beginning of a global conflict that would cause the deaths of approximately forty-five million people.

There were other major and occasionally violent eruptions, as well: the end of Spain's Civil War, Russia's bloody invasion of Finland and its bloodless conquest of the Baltic states. Italy seized Albania.

The outbreak of war overshadowed all other events, but life went on. The U.S. celebrated a World's Fair in New York and San Francisco. Joe Louis defended his heavyweight boxing title by beating Tony Galento. Movie fans had a feast of classics, including "The Wizard of Oz" and "Gone With the Wind." The big book event of the year was the publication of John Steinbeck's *The Grapes of Wrath.*

In 1940, the German juggernaut swallowed up Norway, Denmark, Belgium, The Netherlands and France. Hitler turned his full attention to a battered Britain — only 20 miles distant from occupied France. It hardly seemed possible that England could survive, without allies, with an army much reduced and almost without arms after the rescue at Dunkirk.

At this point, Winston Churchill came to power and with eloquent speeches, and a trickle of help from the U.S., he steeled his country's courage for the long battle to come.

With the winds of war at his back, President Franklin Roosevelt was elected to an unprecedented third term, defeating the unconventional Republican candidate, a non-politician, Wendell Willkie.

The exiled Russian revolutionary, Leon Trotsky, was murdered in Mexico.

Americans clung to their diversions. Jimmy Demaret won the Masters golf tournament, trailed by two other Texans, Lloyd Mangrum and Byron Nelson. Bob Feller, Cleveland's 21-year old fireballer, pitched a no-hitter on opening day. A seven-year old horse named Seabiscuit became racing's alltime biggest money-maker. Ernest Hemingway published his novel about the Spanish Civil War, *For Whom the Bell Tolls*.

Then it was 1941, and just seeing or hearing that year creates a mental newsreel of events that changed the world. In Houston, people were leaving church, sitting down to lunch, or finishing the Sunday papers when the news crackled across the radio:

On December 7th, without warning, the Japanese bombed the American military base at Pearl Harbor. Their planes numbered 360, launched from aircraft carries that were part of a naval armada that had sailed undetected across the Pacific. The dive bombers came in from the southeast over Diamond Head, and their torpedoes devastated most of a U.S. fleet trapped in the harbor. The battleship, the *Arizona*, went down with all hands.

I knew that within a year, my life and my law career were going to be put on hold. The United States was at war, and the war was everything.

Private Fred Parks, shortly after enlisting.

Section IV

Military Justice
December 1942 to September 1945

Receiving the Bronze star from the commanding officer, 15th Air Force, in 1945.

Chapter 4

The Last Good War

IT IS FAIRLY EASY now, fifty years later, to think about World War II and feel almost nostalgic; the last good war, people keep saying. It was a romantic time, with stirring war movies, weepy songs and memories of faraway places; the Andrews Sisters, bond rallies and gas rationing.

But the war was real and it was bloody and the good part was simply that our side won and it brought the country together as never before, and never again.

I made up my mind to enlist and there was little soul-searching about it because I loathe a draft dodger. There was a kind of jubilation about going off to war. You were too full of the flag to worry about what might go wrong. Wars no longer hold much glamour for us, not after Korea and Vietnam, but it is probably a good thing that we felt that way once.

If you served, you didn't have to explain why. But I remember this deathless line from the speech by

General Patton to the Third Army on the eve of D-Day: " . . . and when you are sitting at the fire with your grandson on your knee, and he asks you what you did in the Great World War II, you won't have to say, 'I shoveled shit in Louisiana.'"

That was surely one of the reasons, a pretty convincing one, for giving up whatever it was we left behind.

I enlisted as a private in the Army Air Force on December 1, 1942, attached to the advanced flying school at the Brooks Air Force Base in San Antonio. I was Private J. Fred Parks, Serial Number 18230696.

With my law experience, I was assigned to the Judge Advocate section of the base, under a Major Michaels. I had a bunk in the enlisted men's barracks, where everyone slept in a double-decker bunk except the sergeant, who had a small, separate room, at one end of the barracks.

Major Michaels had told me that there were no promotion slots in his department, but he had negotiated an agreement with the commanding officer of the base. He had a commitment that anybody who worked in the Judge Advocate's section would get first preference to attend Officer Candidate School.

Michaels was an attorney, but had never practiced law, so he delegated me to be his unofficial advisor, and he frequently asked my advice on the handling of certain court martials.

Two cases come quickly to mind. In one, a considerable amount of valuables, watches, rings and other valuables, had been stolen. He asked me how he should go about investigating the thefts. I told him the way I would do it would be to visit the pawn shops in the area, an idea he liked so much he assigned me the job. I had a car and called on all the pawn shops in the San Antonio area. If I ran into any resistance, I had no problem in saying that I would take it up with the authorities at the base. I assured them the Army could, and would, inspect their property. We finally found some of the missing items and were able through these civilian sources to catch the culprit and convict him.

In another trial, a man claimed he was cut very badly on the arm in a fight started by another soldier. During a recess, Michaels asked me what kind of questions I would ask. I told him I would have the man roll up his sleeve to see the severity of his injury. He did. The man had no scar at all and was convicted of being responsible for the altercation.

In due time, I decided I wanted to go to Officers Candidate School (OCS). My name was processed and I was promoted to corporal and accepted. In preparation for my transfer, I was extended the privilege of using the officer's handball court. With that exercise, and the frequent marching we did, I had rounded into decent shape by the time I reported to Miami, Florida.

The class there lasted three months — you were referred to, after graduation, as a "90-day Wonder." You went in as an enlisted man and came out as a second lieutenant. Another candidate in my class was Don Budge, one of the great tennis players of that era.

At Officers Candidate School, we were required

to rise at 5:30 A.M., dress, hurry outside and line up in formation for roll call, all in a matter of ten to fifteen minutes. Then we could go back to the barracks, shower, shave and get ready to march to the dining hall for breakfast. Everywhere we marched it was in formation, with all of us singing. Our days consisted of classes in various Army procedures, and classes in physical education.

Between meals, we were always hurrying to get into formation, and march back to our classes or to our assigned areas. We were then given assignments, which often kept us busy far into the night. We were under pressure practically every waking minute of the day and evening.

On weekends, we would have parades and would march past a reviewing stand to show our respect to the commanding officers, and the colors. We were also introduced to the .45 automatic pistol, the sidearm of choice for military police and intelligence officers.

At the end of thirty days, you advanced into the next thirty-day class, and after the third one you graduated. You usually were assigned to a good many separate duties. My assignment in the third month was to serve on the Ethics Committee and also to handle complaints against soliders who had violated the rules.

One of the rules that was adhered to strictly involved the Sunday parade, which often followed a Saturday night leave. You stood at attention for a long period of time during the Sunday ceremonies, and if you fainted or passed out, they would have you up on charges for misconduct. If it developed that you had been drinking in the last 24 hours, you would be punished.

I soon learned that the people who were actually taking your name and bringing charges against you were allowed a certain amount of money to buy drinks, on the government, so they would be in the same environment. I learned to go to more expensive bars and was never bothered.

Eventually, we graduated from the Air Intelligence School and I was assigned to Pocatello, Idaho, later to become a part of the Fifth Wing of the 15th Air Force, which would be stationed at Bari, Italy. I went from Idaho to Harrisburg, Pennsylvania, and in between I spent two weeks of my leave visiting friends in Houston.

At Harrisburg, I was assigned to a colonel who was an ex-FBI agent whose services the army had requested. He taught in the school for awhile and was awaiting orders overseas, where he would supervise the protection of military installations, in particular those where ammunition and fuel were to be stored. He was writing a handbook on plant protection and assigned me to write one of the chapters. I subsequently lost the book and have never been able to locate another one.

When we were ready to start classes, the colonel called in his men, most of them second lieutenants, and gave us a little party. He was not in uniform, and I asked if he was not going to wear a gun, what kind of protection would he have. He had a swagger stick, which had a button on it. When he pressed the button, a piece of fine steel would whip out, capable of impaling more than one man at a time.

Immediately after the colonel's departure from Harrisburg, we began our classes, which lasted 55 minutes with five minutes out of each hour to transfer to another class. This was the finest military school that I ever attended. Among the rules in the compound, rank did not count. In other words, a second lieutenant would have the same rights as a one-star general. In particular, this rule applied when you went to mail call. No officer, because of his higher rank, could buck the line ahead of men of lesser rank. I was close to the head of the line one day when a lieutenant colonel popped into the mailroom, took one look at the length of the line and went straight to the window, gave his name and asked if he had any mail. He was handed a letter. An officer of higher rank asked him if he were not instructed, when he checked in, that his rank had no privilege. The lieutenant colonel said he was in a hurry. He was told to go to his room, pick up his belongings, and by that time his orders would be cut transferring him out of the unit. There was no appeal. The man was immediately discharged from the school.

We had many, many problems to address and one of the things that was compulsory was reading *The New York Times*, copies of which were stacked free of charge. You were graded upon some of the articles that appeared in each day's edition.

One of my instructors recommended me for a teaching position at the school, but I was turned down because I graded poorly on one question in an examination, which was a serial-answer question. If you did not get the first answer correctly, the others would not be correct.

Finally, the order came down for each student at the school to be interviewed. There was a buzz around the base that day, each candidate asking what was going on? They were interviewing and grading us to determine whether we would be assigned to overseas duty, or remain in the States. Some of those assigned overseas were quite upset. When I went in for my interview, being a second lieutenant, I saluted, and the officer in charge, a general, asked me if I smoked. I said, yes, and he invited me to light up and have a seat.

They questioned me about many things, then asked the $64,000 question: how do you feel about going overseas? I replied: "Gentlemen, when I complete this course, having been taught how to properly brief a group of men, one of which might be my brother if I had one, and I had gotten as good an understanding of the protection offered him by the service, I will go anywhere the army wants to send me."

The interview ended. Subsequently, I was notified that upon graduation I would return to Pocatello, Idaho, for training with the 777th Squadron, a part of the 464th Bomb Group, which was the intelligence wing of the 15th Army Air Force in Italy.

At Pocatello, I was appointed as the assistant intelligence officer for the squadron. My immediate superior was a man by the name of Dave Camera, from New York, who had been an All-American tackle at Dartmouth and later a ghost writer for Phil Rizzuto, the ex-Yankee turned sportscaster. We hit it off well, and began to act as a unit in briefing missions that were flown in parts of the U. S. and Canada.

At this point, it might be well to describe how the 15th Air Force was organized. There were four bomber groups under the direction of Major General Nathan F. Twining, beginning with the 464th. These made up the 55th Wing, all flying the B-14 bomber.

Their primary targets were the oil fields of Ploesti, Roumania. These fields were of critical importance because they furnished a considerable portion of the oil for the German war machine. Although Ploesti would be our primary target, our bomber group, the 464th, flew missions to other targets ranging from Berlin to Vienna to Northern Italy.

But the deadly excitement of the air war was still some weeks in the future for those of us training at Pocatello. I would soon find myself involved in a couple of grim assignments and one or more controversies.

One of our crews had gone down in the mountains in the dead of winter, and we were sent out to find them. Having had experience in South Dakota, working out in the snow-covered areas, I covered my cheeks with the black of a cork, which cut the glare of the sun, and we flew for several hours — along with other search planes — until the missing aircraft was spotted. We took the proper coordinates and locations and returned to the base. A rescue team went out, but sadly all the crewmen were dead and the plane badly damaged.

It was my reluctant duty on two occasions to accompany the body of one of the dead crew members to his home, and pay the respects of the air force to the family. This was in every way an unpleasant duty, and I found no consolation in performing it.

Still, you could accept almost any hazard of war, except pettiness. There was one major known to be especially overbearing, who really wanted to demonstrate his authority, so I marked him as someone I might have trouble with in the future.

One night, when I was on CQ (the officer in charge of quarters), I went through the personnel files and learned that he had been a used car salesman in civilian life. Although he had achieved the rank of major, he had been in considerable trouble both in and out of the service. He had some lawsuits still pending.

One day, without provocation, he decided to strip a technical sergeant of his stripes for some frivolous reason. I intervened and prevented it. That set the stage for future developments in Italy. In due course, we finished the work at Pocatello and were notified we would be going overseas. However, we did not know where or when.

In our briefing rooms we used plexiglass to put over the maps, which could be wiped off and reused again and again. We would trace on top of them the route of the missions. In packing the equipment, I included a number of sheets of this plexiglass. In addition, I sneaked in some slot machines, which we would put to good use after we landed in Italy.

Eventually, we shipped out of Idaho in the dead of winter on a train for Patrick Henry. We stopped off at Chicago and everything on the train was frozen solid, not quite including the troops. We were permitted to get off at the station and spend the evening on the town until the train was serviced, and we continued our journey to our port of debarkation, Patrick Henry. There we were given a short leave and I went to Washington, D.C. Previously, I had received a communication from a friend of mine stationed in D.C., who told me to look him up if I was ever there. I was not aware at the time that he was involved in duties of some secrecy.

When I arrived in the capital, I went through the telephone book of the officers in the Pentagon and could not find him listed. I then found him in the city directory and called; his wife answered. She said he worked in a not very nice section of the city, and gave me directions. I called to tell him I was on my way over to his office, walked down a series of narrow back streets and knocked on his door. It was opened by perhaps the largest black man I had ever seen. He must have been six-foot-six and weighed 240 pounds, not an ounce of it fat. He asked what I wanted. When I told him, he closed the door, leaving me standing outside.

A few moments later, he came back and I followed him into a room where my friend joined us. I told him I was shipping out and he invited me to meet his superior officer. After some conversation, his superior asked me if I knew where I was going. I told him truthfully that I did not, but that the scuttlebutt had us headed somewhere in Italy.

Whereupon, he turned in his chair and pulled out a map, and there was a line running through Italy. He said to make up a code between my friend and me, and when I got there to let him know on which side of the line — east or west — I would be located. I told him this seemed an unsual request and might I ask why he wanted to know?

He said he was in counter-intelligence, and his territory extended to a certain area of Italy. From what my friend told me, he wanted to enlist me in his operation.

After I arrived in Bari, Italy, I notified him of my location, which turned out not to be within his territory. I would not be hearing from him again.

We had sailed out of Patrick Henry on a Liberty ship in mid-January of 1943 and arrived in Italy some 27 days later. I was in charge of fifty men, some of whom were officers, who were billeted in the psychiatric ward of the ship. Some of the other officers and enlisted men had hanging hammocks in the middle of the vessel, both fore and aft. This was no pleasure cruise.

There was a man so frightened he would not remove any of his clothing. He constantly told me he could see a periscope. I made many trips by sea during the war, but never saw an enemy submarine. When we left the convoy and started on our own for the east side of the Italian boot, this man ran up to me that day and said he had seen a periscope. I was mindful of the little boy who cried wolf, and this was not a warning I could ignore. When we got topside, sure enough, there was a periscope. Then I was the one who began to feel a slight tremble, thinking this could be the end of the line. It turned out to be one of ours and it surfaced to give us messages related to where we were, and our destination — Bari, Italy.

During the Atlantic crossing, we conducted emergency drills in the event we had to evacuate the ship. One day the commanding officer approached me and said we had to find a way to assure that the men would come out on deck. Many of them were ignoring the drills. I asked him what was in the cargo. He said he didn't know. We went to the captain of the Liberty ship and he led us down to the cargo area and showed me our cargo — which consisted of 500-pound bombs in crates, with the fuses attached to the crate.

Using the intercom, I informed the men what was in the hold. The next time we had a drill, the men almost tore the ladders off, trying to get topside.

We finally docked at Brandesi, and while we were attending to other matters the natives came out to sell us wines. Some of the medics called my attention to the stream of garbage flowing out of the city, from which the natives were retrieving bottles, refilling them with wine and selling them again. I told the men there would be no more wine bought or sold, and I explained why.

When we arrived at Pantanella Hill, the officers were assigned four to a tent, sixteen-feet square. In rather short order, we had our quarters shipshape and began preparations for getting the bombers operational. For myself, the crossing had not been made any easier by the fact that I had contracted trench mouth before we left Patrick Henry, and there was no treatment for it.

The first thing I did was see a dentist, and he wanted to yank all of my teeth. I declined, and went to an outfit that was laying the metal matting for the landing strip the bombers would be using. I borrowed some medicine from them, which eased the discomfort for the next three or four days. Then I went to a base hospital and received proper medical attention.

Before we had the Pantanella Hill Airfield in combat order, we operated temporarily off another base. During the time of that operation, they had a number of unexplained plane crashes and later determined that they had been caused by spies and German sympathizers. They would hide a plastic explosive that was controlled by atmospheric conditions, and when the aircraft reached a certain height it blew out the instrument that guided the plane and caused it to crash.

The problem was referred to us and no one seemed to know how to deal with it. Finding and disposing of the explosive was nearly impossible. I began to study the conditions around the flights. There were too many people in the area who had no reason to actually come in direct contact with the planes. No one had tried to bar them because it was a small base, and a large hangar with machine shops and repair shops and the like.

I recommended the posting of signs, in English and Italian, stating that anyone seen near the planes, or in any manner touching a plane, would be shot on sight. Eventually, the problem went away.

There was a delay in getting operational. The landing strip had to be laid, the bombers had to be serviced, maps had to be folded and indexed as to targets. More than one map would have to be supplied to each bomber crew. During this period of time, the enlisted men were confined to base and the officers could leave and go into town.

Headquarters set up an officer's club for the officers of our bomber group. I avoided the club and one day the commanding officer called me and said he noticed that he had not seen me there. He was curious about why I had chosen to stay away. Without saying so, I imagine he thought I was being antisocial. I told him that when I was in the Air Intelligence School in Harrisburg, and again at Officers Candidate School in Miami, they had impressed upon me that the officers were to look after the men of lesser rank. I pointed out that we had a club in which alcohol was consumed, while the enlisted men were restricted to the base. This was contrary to what I had been taught, and as a matter of simple fairness I did not feel it was right for an officer to go out, drink and have fun, and the enlisted men to have nothing. On military grounds, I thought it was bad for morale.

The C. O. asked if I had any suggestions. I told him I would let the enlisted men open a club. He agreed and put me in charge of opening one for the 777th. If it worked out, he said, we would let the other squadrons use it.

I went to the master sergeant (the "Top Kick") of the 777th and told him what had happened. The enlisted men had contributed to a "kitty," to be used for the benefit of them all. I asked him how much money he had in this fund. When he told me, I said, "Let's go buy us a barrel of wine." I took my command car and, after making some rather intensive inquiries through an interpeter, we learned there was a wine cellar up in the mountains that the Germans had failed to locate.

We drove up there and sampled the wine, and bought a barrel of it with their money. Returning to the base, we selected a site for the enlisted men's club, what was left of a bombed out building with walls of white limestone. We made a ceiling for it out of a tent and immediately we had a club. The Top Kick and I figured out, mathematically, that each man would receive a cup of wine (the cup that covered their canteen). I also told him two men would be assigned to maintain order and would be required to stay sober. They would be rewarded with double rations the next day. If anyone got out of line, it was their duty to "cold cock" him and put him to bed. I reasoned that if any disturbance occurred, and was reported, the enlisted men would never have a permanent club.

Only one airman got unruly and was put to bed in the proper fashion. Eventually, the commanding officer declared the experiment was a success. He explained to the other three squadrons how it worked and they built similar clubs.

The CO asked if I was satisfied and I said, no, there was another matter. The enlisted men should have one of our two-way radios. We had several in our supplies, at a cost of about $750 each, and you could either send or receive. The CO said that was not a problem. He called the supply sergeant and said he needed a radio. A startled look crossed his face and I heard him ask, gruffly, "Well, where are they?"

He listened unhappily, turned to me and said, "They've been issued to all the officers." So it was a problem, after all, but I pointed out that most of the officers were quartered in tents sixteen-foot square, so it hardly seemed necessary to have a radio in each one.

The next day the enlisted men got their radio.

This sort of concern for the men's entertainment, and thirst, may seem misplaced given the gravity of war. But I can tell you, tedium and boredom are also your enemies across the trenches. And it takes a certain amount of high octane fuel to keep the men, as well as the machinery, ready for battle.

We were almost ready to become operational, and my immediate superior was the major I had clashed with back in Pocatello, Idaho (the one who wanted to court martial an enlisted man over a trivial matter and I had intervened.) There was still a tension between us.

The major was responsible for briefing the crews of the 464th Bombing Group, and interrogating them on their return from missions. He assumed the duty of briefing the officers himself, and assigned me to the enlisted men, which was done separately.

The day the maps were brought in, neither of us knew exactly what to do with them. I went to one of the navigators and asked how the maps should be folded. The next day, mine were all folded properly and the major's were not. His looked like a butcher had wrapped a pound of sliced salami in them. Of course, he blamed me for not telling him how to fold the maps. In truth, I wasn't trying to show him up; the incident simply illustrated, I thought, that he was not the type to demean himself by asking a question. In business, that attitude is merely stupid. In war, it can be deadly.

One day, he called me and said, "What information are you giving the enlisted men that I don't give the officers?"

I said I didn't know what he told the officers, but this is what had gotten his attention: The enlisted men had been apprehensive about the amount of time they would be exposed to flak from the enemy guns. We had no directives on such matters, but I told them we would try to devise a method that would determine how long they would be in the flak areas.

With the assistance of other officers, and the information available, we determined the number of anti-aircraft battery at a given target and the approximate time our planes would be in their range. I asked the enlisted men to check it against their watches, which could be hacked — that is, set to give a measured time. We ended up with good estimates of how long they would be subject to this particular danger.

They passed on the time frame to the officers, who informed the major, which led to his query about my briefings. He then issued an order putting the officers and enlisted men together and we took turns briefing them.

The preparations for becoming operational were intense and, as I recall, at one point we worked about thirty-six hours without sleep. We completed the arrangements and briefed the fliers. They had taken off to bomb the target. Everyone was permitted to go to our tents and take a nap. We were told we would be awakened when the crews started returning so they could be debriefed.

I went to my tent, took off my shoes, loosened my collar and laid down on my bed. Five or six hours later, although it seemed like minutes, I was awakened and told to report back to the office.

After the debriefing was completed, I was approached by a friend, Andy, who was the escape and evasion officer for the bomb group. He said he had gone back to sleep after being awakened, and the major had told him he intended to press charges against him. He asked me what could be done. I offered to represent him if the case went to court-martial.

He was visibly relieved. He said he needed someone and would appreciate it the rest of his life. That ended the matter until a day or so later.

I was shaving in the officers' lavatory, which had running water and half a roof. I was alone when the commanding officer walked in. He could have stood anywhere he wanted, but he took the mirror next to mine. He called me by name and we exchanged a few pleasantries. Finally, the CO said he wanted to ask me a question. What sort of officer, he asked, was my superior at the 777th Squadron?

I waited a minute or so and asked him if he wanted a military answer or a civilian one? He smiled at the distinction and said to give him the civilian answer. I told him the major was a sorry, no good S.O.B. I explained what had happened in Pocatello and what he was doing to Andy, who had rolled over and gone back to sleep an extra ten or fifteen minutes after being up for thirty-five consecutive hours.

The CO thanked me. No court martial papers were ever issued against Andy.

I knew there was going to be a day of reckoning between the major and me. I didn't know when or over what issue, but it didn't take psychic powers to see it coming.

We proceeded with our briefing duties, and I was sent to Bari, Italy, for one week to attend the Trial Judge Advocate's school. I had, coincidentally, applied for this course when we were stateside, but it was not available to me. Now, I was assigned to try any court martial cases for our wing. It was impersonal work, with one exception.

I received a complaint against an enlisted man who had, contrary to military orders, written a letter to his family telling them he was still at Panatella Hill, but would be shipping out soon, probably to Italy. The CO called me to his tent and said he wanted me to draw up the charges and prosecute the man.

I asked him to let me play devil's advocate and make the case why I didn't think the charges ought to be filed. I explained that, in the first place, we got here safely so the information the airman wrote in his letter did no harm. Secondly, it would be an onerous burden to try the case. The man did not have to testify and incriminate himself.

The general said, "I've got the letter."

True, I said, but as a practical matter I still could not prosecute him. I would have to be able to identify everyone who touched the letter after he dropped it in the mailbox, including the postman who delivered it, to establish the chain of possession before it got into the general's hands. By that time, the war could be over.

The general shook his head and said, there was no way we could go to those lengths. I said that was the point I was trying to make. I recommended that he call in the airman and reprimand him and then forget about it.

I had no hesitation about trying someone who broke the law or the rules. I certainly wasn't opposed to military discipline or tradition. It was military pettiness I couldn't abide.

On May 6, 1944, our bomber group flew its first in a series of missions, whose objective was the systematic destruction of the oil refinery and rail transport facilities in Rumania. We also targeted the major aircraft plant in the area. Our squadron, having arrived last, did not fly on this mission, but did take part in the next.

That group flew on May 18, and our target was the Ploesti Concordia Vega Refinery. We would not know until later how critical the Ploesti oilfields were to the final victory of the allied forces in Europe.

On the last day in May, 1944, our bombers took out the Wiener-Neustadter complex, a unit that had raised oil to a high priority in Ploesti. The next mission happened to be on D-Day, the sixth of June. While the largest invasion force in history was landing at Normandy, our target was the largest refinery still active in the area, and the adjacent oil storage tanks.

Between mid-May and August 19, 1944, some

two dozen large scale raids were launched against Ploesti, deep inside Rumania, north of Bucharest, the capital. Earlier raids had been attempted in mid-1942 from air bases in Libya, a 3,000-mile round trip. The fields had been heavily fortified by the Germans and these raids, using B-24 Liberators, were considered almost suicide missions. It wasn't until we began to hammer at them from Italy all through the spring and summer of '44 that we succeeded in shutting down this strategic target.

I am probably among a handful of people who have been fortunate enough to retain the official Air Force record, "The Air Battle of Ploesti," which includes this foreword by Major General Nathan F. Twining:

"A little over six months ago — on 19 August 1944 — the last of twenty-four heavy blows was delivered to the then Axis-held Roumanian oil refineries at Ploesti. This was the climax of one of strategic air power's greatest triumphs, a five-month aerial campaign carried out by bombers and fighters of the Mediterranean Allied Strategic Air Force based in Italy. The overall effect of Ploesti's loss to the enemy is becoming more noticeable every day ... on the battlefields of Europe, where a battered Wehrmacht is fast losing its mobility; in the air over Germany, where the Luftwaffe is virtually grounded; in the core of German inudstrial economy — all for lack of gasoline and oil so vital in the now hopeless fight against the ring of steel closing ever tighter around the heart of Germany.

"The narratives which follow, the analytical studies set forth ... the many photographs, charts and statistics round out a portrait of the Air Battle of Ploesti

. . . The Battle will long be remembered by the airmen who won it, by the ground echelons which sustained it, by the many men and women of the armed forces who in different ways supported it, by the people of the United Nations whose victory was brought closer because of it, and above all by the enemy whose certain defeat was carved deeply in the charred ruins of the Ploesti oil refineries."

/s/N.F. Twining
Major General, USA
Commanding

THE AIR BATTLE OF PLOESTI

Five miles above the rolling plains of Roumania was waged between 5 April and 19 August 1944 one of the decisive battles of World War II — a five-month, bitterly contested fight to eliminate Ploesti, the greatest single source of oil available to the Axis. This was a unique campaign, peculiar to the times and rendered possible by the supreme equipment and productive capacity of the United Nations, and above all by the courage and resourcefulness of a group of intrepid airmen who would not be beaten. The battle of Ploesti was an air battle, carried on principally by huge fleets of American four-engine bombers, penetrating deep inside enemy territory, bringing the attack to the heart of the German war machine and striking hard at its most vital installations.

During the campaign, the U. S. Fifteenth Air Force based in Italy sent 5,446 bombers against Ploesti in twenty daylight missions, dropped 13,286 tons of bombs and succeeded long before the Russian occupation (late in August 1944) in denying Germany a major portion of the fuel, without which air forces cannot fly, modern mechanized armies are unable to move, and industry bogs down. Four of the twenty-four attacks on Ploesti were night missions, successfully executed by 229 Wellingtons, Halifaxes and Liberators of the 205 Group, RAF, which with the U. S. Fifteenth Air Force, comprises the Mediterranean Allied Strategic Air Force. These attacks contributed substantially to the overall success of the campaign.

Ploesti had been struck twice before in 1942 and 1943 by Middle East based B-24's of the American Air Forces. One of these attacks was the now famous tree-top attack by B-24's which flew . . . from Libyan bases. Successful as it was, this attack could not at that time be repeated. Not until heavy bombers could be based within a reasonable, operational radius of Ploesti would it be possible to destroy again and again, and finally to prevent production of the great oil refineries.

The successful invasion of Italy in September 1943 and the subsequent advance of the Allied ground forces, opened up the plains of Foggia — a natural airfield on the East coast of the Italian peninsula. Early in December 1943 the Fifteenth Air Force commenced operations from Italy, taking part in the ground campaign and in the counter-air program designed to knock the Luftwaffe (the German Air Force) out of the sky — the top priority assignment for the United States Strategic Air Forces in Europe. As early as March the future programs for heavy daylight bombers based in Italy and England had become clear.

February's operations had rocked German aircraft production to its foundations and subsequent attacks by Allied bombers had further increased the strain on the enemy's air defenses . . .

It was time to initiate the all-out air assault on Germany's military, industrial and economic life — for which destruction of the enemy's fighter defense had been a necessary preparation. Gasoline production constituted the weakest link in the German war machine. As a target system it offered a relatively limited number of objectives, vulnerable to air attack, which could be readily identified and not easily dispersed. Oil products were essential to all phases of the enemy's war effort, and his stocks were known to be low.

Thirty per cent of all Axis oil production was concentrated at Ploesti . . . within range of the Fifteenth Air Force and not open to attack by any other Allied military organization.

Thus the stage was set for what was to become strategic air power's greatest single contribution to the ultimate destruction of the Wehrmacht. Eight months after the 1943 attack, the first of 24 hammer blows was delivered to Ploesti on 5 April 1944. Although this attack and the four that followed were by directive aimed at the Ploesti rail yards running through the heart of the oil refineries, so severe was the damage to the adjacent oil installations that the desirability and effectiveness of serial bombardment of oil refineries was no longer questioned. Oil became at once the top strategic priority. It was not only a way to cripple the enemy's war machine prior to the invasion of the European continent, but also the most effective means of keeping the German Air Force in check.

... No one realized the significance of the Ploesti bombing more than the enemy. His efforts to defend the refineries are ample testimony to the importance of this objective. After the first few attacks, the Germans found that (their) aerial defense would not stop the seemingly never ending stream of bombers and their cargoes of destruction. The bombers were armed "to the teeth," their gunners could shoot as well as their bombardiers could pinpoint targets. Added to the destruction of this fighter force by bombers and their escorting fighters was the inability of the enemy to provide replacement aircraft at a rate equivalent to his losses.

Heavy guns were constantly added to the Ploesti flak ring. Nowhere on the contintent could be found a more accurate or deadly concentration of "those little black flowers that bloom in the sky." Losses to flak were high, but not prohibitive, and still the bombers came, adding almost daily to the destruction of precious oil. What proved to be the enemy's most successful defensive technique was a smokescreen to hide the refineries from the keen eyes of the Norden and Sperry bombsights.

This new tactic temporarily slowed up the inevitable loss of Ploesti as an oil source, but it was defeated through the development of successful counter-measures. For almost five months the battle continued. A grand total of 9,173 aircraft (including

5,409 heavy bombers) dropped 13,663 tons of bombs, knocked down 360 enemy fighters — and destroyed Ploesti.

Thus did General Twining introduce the story of one of the war's great air victories. Of course, numbers alone can't begin to tell the human dimensions of these raids. There were countless examples of devotion to duty and heroism over enemy territory — and as many more that would never be known. A bombardier gave up his parachute to a wounded gunner and pushed him to safety through the open bomb bay of a Flying Fortress. Last seen, the bombardier was standing alone on the catwalk. Seconds later, the ship went into a spin from which it never recovered.

The general gave credit elsewhere: to the crew chiefs and the men of the "line," then added: "It must not be overlooked that before an aircraft ever leaves the ground there has to be a plan — detailed and accurate in every respect. Crews must be furnished all the available and most recent information. Responsible for this are the planning staffs whose closed-door conferences have but one aim — to strike the enemy's most essential installations and to perfect the operating plans that enable our bombing formations to reach and hit the targets without losses out of proportion to the damage accomplished.

" . . . Through the unceasing efforts of all concerned and the spirit of men who were willing, if need be, to sacrifice their lives, the Air Battle of Ploesti was decisively won."

We sent the crews on countless other missions,

including the submarine pens of northern Italy and to targets in Vienna and Berlin. We were aware at all times that if our information was faulty, if the plans went wrong, the results could be gruesome.

One mission over Berlin ended in near disaster. The planes ran out of fuel and had to clear the Alps and land wherever they could. It was at least a week before headquarters could drop the men and supplies to get them home. Had the Germans known of our distress, they could have selectively destroyed the 15th Air Force by blowing up the planes on the ground throughout Italy.

At one of the other wings that flew B-17s, the planes had been heavily damaged by anti-aircraft fire but all of them managed to get back to the base and land. Some had holes in them so big you could have driven a jeep through them. Although there were crewmen who had been wounded, none of them lost their lives.

There is a foreboding in war that many of us would never experience otherwise, and a distrust of anything new. Radar was more or less in its infancy in those days, and we were notified that our squadron was being assigned two men who had been trained in this technology. They would have to fly separately to reduce the risk of losing all of our radar expertise in one crash.

I briefed them for their first mission, whose ultimate target was the industrial city of Vienna. Our orders were only to bomb if the skies were overcast and the crew could not make a visual contact — so they could use the so-called "mickey," or radar scope. The bombardiers dropped their loads as instructed and returned to their bases. It was not until the next morning that we were able to get any confirmation, and by that time the crews were in a fairly heated debate with the radar experts.

According to the reconnaissance photographs, the bombs had missed the targets by seven and a half miles. One of the experts was explaining that the error was the result of how the men had interpreted what they saw on the scope. When lines appeared, this indicated — to the experts — that they were flying over steel structures. Our regular bombardiers, veterans of many a mission, insisted that someone misread the lines because they had flown over heavy forests.

The experts were wrong. They had bombed the hell out of the Vienna woods, seriously depleting the squirrel population. Very shortly, the experts, with the assistance of other senior officers, were able to teach the bombardiers how to read the scopes and bomb the targets they intended to bomb.

Our briefings were rarely routine, although the scene itself was not unlike what you probably remember from the movies: an officer stands at an easel, yanks into place a large map, points out the target, reflects on how some of the men won't make it back and expresses his regret that he can't be with them.

After one briefing, my friend Andy said that someone had been opening the Escape and Evasion kits and pilfering from them. The kits were small, ten inches long by four inches wide and a half-inch thick, wrapped in an oilskin that would stick together, so you had to peel it apart so it would open. They contained a gold-sealed packet of American money that a downed flier could use to buy his freedom. There were silk handkerchiefs with maps printed on them, and fountain pens that doubled as a compass when they hung correctly.

The kits were issued to the men at each briefing before daylight and turned in after they came back from a mission. We had two hundred in our inventory and thirty to forty had been opened and the money and other elements were missing. The commanding officer, a West Point man, was at a loss as to how to deal with the problem. I asked his permission to make a special announcement at the next briefing, and thought I could end the problem of having the kits being vandalized.

I told the men, "Some sons of bitches among you have been opening the kits and stealing from them. The money they took was to help you survive if you were unfortunate enough to get shot down." I was not eligible to fly on any missions because I was not rated. But I added, "If I was flying and I saw someone fooling around with my Escape and Evasion packet I would just push his ass out the plane and report him missing in action."

The CO, being a West Point man, almost dragged me off the platform. He said I couldn't tell these men to kill each other. I told him I bet we wouldn't have any more thefts — and we didn't.

A short time after we became operational, the Wing headquarters sent a man to our group and advised all of the officers that they could have a fifth of whiskey with a limit of two per man at two dollars per bottle. All or most of us signed up and a considerable length of time passed before the whiskey was delivered. It was enjoyed by those who were still among us.

But many who had signed up either had been shot down or completed their missions and gone home (a tour consisted of fifty missions; some were counted as double.) When the second offer to buy whiskey was made, very few orders were placed.

The special services clerk was bewildered by the prospect of having to account for the allotment of the men who were gone. I offered to buy whatever was left unsold, and I wound up with a good many cases of whiskey. I promptly had a locker box made with a padlock to hold my supply. As trading material, this was better than chocolates and almost as good as nylon stockings.

About this time, the commanding officer notified me that I had been transferred to the headquarters of the 15th Air Force to serve in the Trial Judge Advocate's office. I packed my things, including my whiskey, took my jeep and drove to Bari, Italy, to begin this assignment.

In Bari, I had an apartment downtown. The Air Force had requisitioned the Yacht Club as a deluxe mess hall, serving three meals a day to all headquarters personnel and their guests. The use of a jeep came with my new job, and it was impressed on me that it needed to be parked in a secure area, or it would be stolen or stripped. Any damages had to be paid out of your own pocket. I walked much of the time simply to avoid parking in areas that were not secure.

There were days when the war seemed far away. A captain I knew (I was still a lieutenant) approached me and said, casually, "Fred, I understand you have quite a bit of American liquor." He said he needed to entertain his superior officer, whose support he wanted for a future assignment. He asked if he could bring him over for a drink? I said, of course.

The next day he brought his major to my apartment. I asked what they would like and opened three cabinets filled with liquor. The major said, "Goddamn, you must be in the black market." I quickly assured him, "No, I just own it. I don't sell it." I gave him a bottle as a gift. My friend got his favor and I knew if I needed help I could call on him.

But I wasn't running a saloon. The cases began to come with increasing frequency and there was little time for entertainment.

I walked out of the Yacht Club one day after lunch and, to my surprise, there stood Dave Camera, who had been my boss at Pocatello, Idaho. We climbed into his jeep and drove to the office. He asked if it was true that a man facing a court martial had the right to select anyone in the command as his defense counsel. I said, yes, that was so. "Well," he said, "I have a problem and I want you to represent me."

This was his story: he had been with a group in northern Italy that was scheduled to be rotated home fairly soon. At a tag dance one night, he was dancing with a nurse when the commanding officer, a West Point man, cut in on him. After a considerable lapse of time, Dave cut in on the colonel, who refused to surrender the lady. Dave remarked that everyone there was an officer and they were honor bound to respect the custom. The colonel reacted by putting Dave under house arrest.

The episode served as a wonderful reminder that even in the midst of this great and bloody adventure, even as the 8th Army moved with all possible speed to gain the Adriatic coast, there was time for callous and petty behavior.

Dave reported as ordered the next morning. The colonel gave him a tongue-lashing in front of another officer. Then he made a mistake: a demeaning reference to Dave's family and his upbringing. As it happened, Camera was from a fine family in the east. Whereupon, Dave reached over and picked up the court martial papers on the desk. He told the colonel he didn't have grounds to charge him, but maybe this would give him some. He promptly ripped up the documents and let them scatter to the floor. Then he headed to Bari, where he knew I was stationed.

With those facts in mind, I cleared it with my superior and we drove to Dave's base. He had told me that the officer who was present would give us a statement. I took the officer's testimony and told Dave he had nothing to worry about, but to hold his temper. I requested an audience with the colonel (I was by then a captain) and informed him I was the Trial Judge Advocate for the 15th Air Force and, under the rules, Officer Dave Camera had requested that I defend him in the court martial proceedings.

The colonel said, fine, because he was sure as hell going to court martial him.

At that point, I suggested he should reconsider. He said, under no circumstances would he reconsider.

It was time to bring out the brass knuckles. I said, "Sir, you're a West Point man, regular army. When you disparaged Dave's family, and his upbringing, you breached the conduct expected of a superior officer. An incident like this will appear in your 201 file (his service record) forever . . . and it would be quite detrimental to you in your future advancements."

He denied making such remarks. With a flourish, I pulled out the statement of the officer who had been in the room at the time Dave tore up the papers. I read it aloud. That took the wind out of him. I advised him to cut new orders assigning Dave to another outfit, and that would be the end of it.

Dave was transferred out, and that was the last time we saw each other. We did stay in touch by phone. Dave lived in Rye, New York, had been a football star at Dartmouth before the war and helped co-author a book with Phil Rizzuto, the shortstop on the great Yankee teams of the '40s and '50s.

The abiding difference between military and civilian cases is not in the legal standards, but in the emotional ones. You are aware at all times that men are being tried who could be, or have been, asked to make sacrifices for their country. In some instances, the witnesses whose testimony may support or damage their cases, have bonded with them. As with the police, you may have sympathy for the difficult jobs they do, or you may hold them to a higher standard.

I encountered some or all of these conflicts in the variety of cases I tried:

— There was a constant battle against those who see war as a sort of free enterprise zone. One airman had a lucrative business going on the side. His family sent him regular deliveries of five-pound packages, which were never opened in the States. Each appeared to contain a carton of cigarettes. Instead, the packs had been opened and stuffed with cotton and held lighter flints. At that time, in Italy, the Post Exchange sold all kinds of cigarette lighters, but very few flints. What was worth about a nickel back home, he was selling for a dollar.

He had people in his outfit go to different cities in the north and south of Italy to deliver these flints, and wire the money — less their cut — to his family in the States. He might have made it safely through the whole war, except that one of the cartons was mishandled in transportation, and the military mail handlers then tracked the money transmissions. He was arrested and charged.

He had made literally thousands of dollars. But I doubt if there was much left by the time he was available to enjoy it.

— Fifty years later, it is hard to realize that the United States fought and won a war with a military force that was almost totally segregated. In the 464th Bomber Group there was not a single black. I assume that the other bomber groups that made up the 15th Air Force were of a similar construction.

The black G.I.'s made up most of the trucking

and transportation units, with the exception of their white officers. The trucks delivered the bombs, equipment, supplies and provisions that kept every unit rolling.

Along the same lines, the rest camps in which personnel were allowed to spend their furloughs were also segregated. The 15th Air Force attempted to further segregate the rest camps in northern Italy, just below the Alps. When I was in the Trial Judge Advocate's office, I was requested to write an opinion as to whether or not the funds contributed by all Air Force officers in the 15th Air Force could be used for an exclusive rest camp for field grade officers only. (Field grade being majors and above.) I wrote an opinion that it could not be so restricted because they were using funds contributed by first and second lieutenants and captains, and using it for a select few. Therefore, they had to accept officers of lesser rank than field grade.

In keeping with the system, there was a rest camp operated entirely by black personnel and attended only by black personnel. It was only after the war that this segregation among the troops was corrected by legislation, and by an executive order of President Truman.

In one of the thorniest cases of that war zone, a complaint was lodged against the major who commanded the camp — brought by his second in command, a captain and a former Pennsylvania highway patrolman.

It developed that the major and the camp chaplain had Italian girl friends, and the major favored the ladies by allowing them to go home (to Naples) in a military vehicle, and they were given supplies out of the PX. All of which was illegal.

This tidy arrangement was undone because, as often happens in such affairs, the woman who slept with the major began to flex her importance. She would get the enlisted men to run her errands with the words, *"Mi Majore"* — do what I say or the major will get after you.

One day she encountered the former highway cop and ordered him to drive her back to camp. He said no. She threatened him and warned that the major would deal with him when they got back. Sure enough, the major called him in and said he would transfer him out of that outfit. He had the orders cut.

The captain took his jeep and drove to his former base and talked to his former commander, a white colonel. The report began its climb up the chain — from the captain to the colonel to our general, and then back down the ranks to my superior officer, a Major Larry Long.

Long called me in and said I would have to try the case. He did not have to impress upon me that it was more awkward or more sensitive than any other such case. I asked him to let me have the best court reporter I could find, and I would handle it. He agreed.

The captain who filed the complaint was brought to my office and I took a detailed statement from him. Then we got in my car and drove to the rest camp, arriving at around two in the morning. I woke up the major in accordance with military custom, identified myself, and requested quarters for the night, which he provided. I told him I wanted to meet with him in the morning.

Shortly after dawn, we went to his office and I told the major I wanted to interview some of the men who were at the camp. I was in the process of taking statements, with my court reporter, when in walked General Benjamin Davis, the only black general in the European theater, and his son, Colonel Benjamin Davis, Jr., who flew P-38's.

The general asked what I was doing and under whose authority I was conducting the investigation. I told him I was acting under the authority of the commanding officer of the 15th Air Force, and that the only way I could withdraw was on a direct order from my commanding officer. Then I explained my presence and told him I was taking statements in response to a complaint against officers in the rest camp. No counter orders were forthcoming. I continued my questioning and in time the case was set for trial.

I understood the discomfort of General Davis. Every advance made by blacks in the military had been measured by inches, and under intense scrutiny. Any misstep, any flaw, made that progress all the more difficult and gave comfort to those determined to resist it. And there were plenty of white officers sharing a bed with the willing ladies of Italy and other war-ravaged countries. But, as far as was known, they didn't let their casual lady friends give commands to their troops.

Once the trial began, as I called each of the black

enlisted men and officers who were at the rest camp, they retracted their statements. Under military law, you could not designate your own witnesses as hostile; therefore, I could not cross-examine them to show they were lying. I saw the case slipping away. We were losing.

At the conclusion of one day's testimony, it was clear in my judgment that the soldiers had been intimidated into denying their original statements. There was nothing I could do about it. I needed someone who would corroborate that the major had slept with the woman; that he had given her favors and provided her with military goods to which she was not entitled.

The captain who had brought the complaint asked how the trial was progressing. I said, not too well and told him the black men who had given me statements had repudiated them on the witness stand. I had no proof of the allegations of misconduct by the major or the captain, who was a man of the cloth. He then asked me what I needed. I said I needed a witness who could preferably place the major in bed with an Italian woman.

He asked if the witness had to be a soldier. I said, no. He said he could get the Italian man who cleaned up the major's apartment to testify. I called the motor pool, which I was authorized to do at any time, gave him the keys to my command car and told him to hurry.

At about noon on the second day after he left, I was out of witnesses and was making double talk to the court, stalling for time. I had been admonished to complete the case. I asked for a recess of thirty minutes to review my notes and I would quickly wind up the case. I went back to my office and was wondering what I was going to do, when I heard the brakes of my command car squeal. I looked out the window and saw the captain with a little Italian man in the passenger seat. I returned to the court and told the judges that I had a witness who had just arrived, and I would put him on the stand and conclude my case. I had not yet had time to interview him, and needed a few more minutes to do so.

The additional time was granted. I questioned the man and learned that he was the Italian custodian who cleaned up the sleeping quarters of the major. He had found the major in bed with his mistress on frequent mornings.

The major was convicted of dereliction of duty, and misuse of government property. The chaplain was also convicted and given a lesser sentence. Later, the defense attorney told me that when the major saw the Italian shuffle into the courtroom, rubbing the edges of his hat, he asked if there was any way to keep that man off the stand? His defense counsel said, "Only if he drops dead before he gets there."

— There are times when you simply can't make excuses for people, for the temptations they may have faced or the circumstances that left them weak or desperate. Sometimes you just have to recognize that you are dealing with a bad apple, someone with no good in them, and they deserve to be hunted down and punished.

Some cases are more satisfying than others. I

court martialed the ringleader of a gang of American soldiers, who had deserted, gone AWOL (Absent Without Leave) and were operating a black market ring in Italy. The ringleader — I'll call him Mister X — was an Italian who had been involved in the moving of trucks in the motor pool in North Africa.

He planned his caper well. He had acquired a lot of official orders and hidden them in his luggage, so that later they could be forged to get the trucks past military check points. As long as they had an official stamp, the trucks could go anywhere they wanted. In Naples, the drivers were allowed to get out on the dock and mill around until the transportation was ready to be moved to the outside. Mr. X walked off the dock carrying his own luggage, hailed the first Italian kid he saw and asked to be guided to a hotel. In an almost Dickensian story, he recruited a band of kids to locate G.I.'s who were AWOL. He would take them back to the hotel, where he had cash, civilian clothes and girls waiting for them.

Later, he would send them to the docks, dressed in military uniforms, with forged orders, and they would sign for new American trucks and drive them off. The trucks would be stored in a garage until they had an opportunity to use them.

The stolen trucks could be rented for the equivalent of $100 a day, so they were making a lot of money when they were finally captured, returned to their outfits and court martialed.

Mister X had a bigtime racket going, until we broke it up and convicted him. You might say he traded down — going from a truck to a prison van and behind bars.

— It would be hard to overstate how big the black market industry was at the time, in a separate orbit around the war. Trucks were the key for the obvious reason — the goods had to be picked up and moved. I had to track down one fellow, who went AWOL and took his truck with him. He had gained a brief notoriety for avoiding capture, as news of his exploits filtered their way back to his old outfit.

He had driven close enough to the German lines to know there would be little if any movement, except for convoys. He concealed the truck in the woods and moved in with an Italian couple, and their attractive daughter. He would slip out at night and forage for anything he could steal and sell. With the help of his buddies back at the motor pool, he was often able to sneak away with a 50-gallon drum of gasoline, which he could sell for a dollar a gallon.

Eventually, he was caught because the Military Police grew suspicious when they got a glimpse of his truck, by then in a condition so grimy and rundown it could hardly stay on the road. When they questioned him, he admitted he was AWOL. He was arrested and taken to Naples where, filled with remorse, he asked to be issued a new uniform and to have his truck overhauled, so he could return to his outfit and accept his punishment. An officer was assigned to accompany him, and he told the prisoner to bring the truck around to the front gate. The fellow got in the truck and headed north and gave them a nice chase before they recaptured him a few days later.

It turned out that he had such a thriving business going in bootleg gasoline, any examination of the records would prove to be a huge embarrassment to the base commanders. When I arrived I was informed that the records, alas, had been burned — in an accidental office fire, so the report said.

We estimated that he had sold thousands of gallons of gasoline on the black market. Exactly how much, we could not determine. He was convicted, although the "fire" no doubt spared a few others from joining him.

— One of the most disturbing cases involved a master sergeant, an army career man, who was an aide to a general — think of Ernest Borgnine in the movie, "From Here to Eternity." He had reached a point where he thought that, with the protection of the general, he was accountable to no one. The general lived in a villa and the top kick would procure whatever he wanted, legal or illegal.

When he went off to a rest camp, he was arrested by the MP's for dealing in the black market. His case was assigned to me for trial, and a court martial board found him guilty and took his stripes away.

An incident was reported to me after he was reduced in rank to private. He walked into the mess hall, where three men jumped him and gave him a brutal beating. An officer who should have been present had conveniently left the hall and gone to the rest room. The soldiers apparently were settling some old scores with the former, high riding master sergeant.

— After VE Day (Victory in Europe), the thought

that was uppermost in everyone's mind was how quickly they could get home. But the wheels of justice didn't stop turning. On a troop ship sailing to New York, a "chicken" colonel was arrested as he stood at the railing, waiting for the anchor to be raised.

It seems he had stumbled over a very basic army regulation: you are responsible for any military property or item assigned to you. The colonel had signed a receipt for a yacht that was requisitioned by the army and docked at a marina in northern Italy. In the closing days of the war, the yacht was destroyed by a fire and the Italian owners filed a claim. They learned that the colonel was the one who had accepted custody of the yacht, and that he was on the verge of shipping out. One thing led to another: he was removed from the ship and sent to our command to testify at a hearing. If found guilty of negligence, he would be court martialed.

Captain Larry Long brought the colonel to my office, introduced us and explained the situation. I told Larry I needed to take an interpreter with me to investigate it. No action had been taken yet against the colonel, and he was able to request a plane to fly us from Bari to the town nearest the rest camp.

We were given a fighter plane and the three of us — the colonel, the translator and myself — squeezed into the cockpit. The pilot was in a world of his own, as pilots sometimes are. He cut quite a few loops, took the plane down to the tops of the large eucalyptus trees, and then did a "peel off" landing, with these results:

I had gotten sick in the back of the plane.

The colonel was mad as hell, wrote down the

name of the pilot, and warned him that if he tried any more of these stunts there would be another court martial, by God.

And after we taxied to the end of the runway, and staggered off the plane, we were met by three or four airport officials who wanted to know who was flying the plane and why he had landed as we did.

We drove to the rest camp on Lake Como, and checked into a small hotel. The colonel called the owner over and told him I was a man who enjoyed fine wine, and to bring me the best bottle he had and he would take care of it. I don't think he was trying to curry favor with me, so much as he was relieved that I was looking into the issues. And his spirits had been lifted by the fact that we had survived the landing.

Carefully, I reminded him that I was in charge of the investigation and he was to treat me with military courtesy, no more or less. The next day, he got back on the plane and returned to Bari, this time without the loops.

My interpreter was a medical school graduate, whose plans to open a practice had been interrupted by the war. I gave him some cash, told him to go down to where the yacht had been docked and talk to everyone he could find about what had happened. I told him to take his time; this was not a frivolous matter, even if it sounded a bit weird. How often do you get a chance to investigate the sinking of a yacht in wartime?

I had about three days of rest, during which I would eat a full breakfast and select a wine for dinner. Then my interpreter came back. He said the facts were these: he had found the man in charge of the yacht, which was used to entertain the officers. They would eat and drink and enjoy a quiet sail on Lake Como at night. In addition, there were several palatial vacation homes on the lake, and the yacht would pull up to their docks and accept invitations from the Americans, English or French who owned or rented the homes.

(I had attended the rest camp myself. I knew an American who owned one of the homes, and was familiar with the routine. With an invitation came a trip to the wine cellar, and a choice of champagne or good wine or whiskey. There would be a case of whatever the guest liked, and an extra bottle waiting to be opened. I estimated that there were hundreds of cases in this man's cellar.)

One night, with the colonel in charge, the yacht had docked and dropped anchor, and the guests had come ashore, retired to their hotel rooms and gone to bed. During the night, the yacht caught fire and was severely damaged. There was no apparent cause for the fire, and guesses ranged from someone failing to put out a cigarette to stray sparks from the stove.

Finally, my interpreter had found the night watchman, who had seen the yacht from shore and was puzzled by a sudden burst of light. He started up a motor boat and headed toward the light. He went aboard and found some kids who were stealing fuel and had knocked over a candle. The yacht caught fire and there was no way to bring it under control.

I prepared my report and went back to headquarters and turned it in. The colonel was exonerated. He dropped by my office and thanked me before he left for the States. This time he was still a passenger when the ship set sail.

By now, the 15th Air Force had shrunk to just a very few people. My superior officer, who was a relatively recent arrival from the States, told me I had more overseas time than the rest of the men in my department and could probably go home anytime I wanted. He was assigned to handle all the claims in Italy growing out of the war, and before he left he officially turned over to me the details of shutting down the 15th Air Force in Italy. I handled the closing and had orders cut to transfer me to another wing.

The last thing I did was to retrieve the photographs that were hanging in my office, a sequence of a plane falling from the skies, and in the final scene the plane is shown flying almost upside down. It crashed with no survivors.

These photographs are significant for two reasons. First, they are uncommon and rare sequential photos showing what happens when an airplane flies through flak, destructs and destroys. This mission was flown over a German installation beyond enemy lines in northen Italy. After the briefing, the technician in the photo lab called me and said that he had a set of pictures I should see. I went down and looked at them and I was struck and moved by them. Knowing that such photographs were routinely destroyed, I took the negatives with me when I left to go to Bari from the bomber group.

During the closing of the 15th Air Force, I had a set of prints made and kept the negatives and brought them home. I was later shocked to find the fourth photograph in a national magazine with a caption that said one crewman had survived.

I called the magazine and asked how they had obtained the picture. They had the name of the man who submitted it, but no phone number or address. I told them that I was the briefing officer on that mission and based upon my checks, there were no survivors and I was surprised that they had published the picture without obtaining confirmation. I can account in only one way for how the pictures found their way to America. When the photo lab reproduced them for me in Bari, the man developing the pictures must have kept a set for himself and sold them to the magazine. They published it because of that extraordinary picture of a plane crash.

But, earlier, arriving at the wing headquarters for processing, I was told again that my orders would be cut and I could go home whenever I wished; my twenty months of overseas service was longer than most of those still on duty.

I had heard rumors that some of the men who were due to be shipped out had been detained on orders that were on file, and their papers were being examined. I actually traded places with an officer who had a lower priority than mine, on the condition that he phone me the day after he arrived and let me know what happened in processing.

We cut his orders and he was so ecstatic to be going home that he packed only a spare uniform and the one he was wearing, and gave the rest away. The next day he called me from Bari. "I'm not going home," he said. "They're looking for lawyers, and they have reassigned me to the Claims Department to help settle any claims made by or against the Italians."

I said, "As many claims as there will be, you better marry an Italian woman, have a son and teach him the law because that's how long it will take to get them settled."

I then obtained permission to make a trip to Naples, taking with me sufficient whiskey to cover any emergency. I found the sergeant in charge of the processing desk, and after a few drinks he told me what they were looking for — lawyers and claims adjustors.

This confirmed my information that some men were being detained, so I went to my commanding officer and told him I wanted to be re-classified. I had shipped out as a combat intelligence officer, which had a different classification number from a Trial Judge Advocate. He cut the orders and re-classified me. In a few days, he requested that I be returned home and I went back to Naples to await transportation to the United States.

In the "Reppie Deppie" (the Replacement Depot), I ran into several friends of mine who knew what I was trying to do. When we went out for dinner, they would make all kinds of remarks about when I was going home. I tried to keep it quiet, but they persisted, and during those two or three days in Naples I spent much of my time at the Officers Club on top of the Orange Palace. I did all the snooping around I could, and I learned that there was really no system; if they found out you were a lawyer they simply grabbed you.

It was a little like the old shipping days when they shanghaied seaman out of the grubbiest bars on the waterfront.

I decided it was time to make my move. I returned to the wing and told the officer in charge that I was ready to go home. He cut the orders and I went back to Naples and was stationed, temporarily, in a building about eight floors high. It had no elevator service because it had been knocked out during the war. We had to walk up and down all those flights and had only a limited amount of water that we could use because it had to be carried up the stairs by hand, in whatever container you could find, a canteen or a cup. So we took our showers on the first floor.

We were there several days and the reason for the delay was a work stoppage back home. At least, that was the story in *Stars & Stripes,* the military newspaper. The paper reported that the dock workers on the East Coast had gone on strike because with the war in Europe now over, they wanted the tonnage they had to lift to be decreased, thus making more work for more people at that critical time. This delayed the reloading of the ships and in turn delayed their trips to pick up more soldiers to be evacuated back to the United States.

We were in the Reppie Deppie for about ten days, and there was nothing to do except see whatever sights were still standing. We went to see Mt. Vesuvius, which had erupted upon our landing twenty months before. We soaked up the scenery, ate, drank and danced at the Orange Palace.

There was always something odd going on. One night as I was returning to my quarters, I saw a jeep sitting in the middle of the street with the engine running, keys in the ignition, and the lights on. I drove the jeep over to the side of the road, turned off the ignition and looked around for the driver. I suppose I waited the better part of an hour before I gave up. I drove the jeep to my barracks and parked it. From that time until I departed for the U.S., I was an exception among those waiting in that I had transportation. The day we left Italy, I turned the keys in to the motor pool together with the jeep and told them how I had acquired it.

Right before we left, an order came down that required everyone to receive a flu shot; there was an epidemic in the States. There were a number of doctors going home, and it was the first time I saw one take a shot (the shots in the units I served in were administered by enlisted men.) This was a powerful shot. About three out of every five men would walk a few steps and then keel over. A lot of the soldiers, particularly the enlisted men, were laughing at the officers, and some doctors, who got their shots and were unable to walk away.

Eventually, we boarded the ship and sailed out of Naples and into the Mediterranean, but in due course the ship changed its direction and headed for North Africa, arriving there in the shank of the evening and tied up at the dock all night. I was curious about that; the thought crossed my mind that perhaps they had found out I had been re-classified, but that was not the case.

The next morning we set sail for the U.S. and after about one hour into the Mediterranean, we turned around and headed back for our starting point. Then I was sure they were going to pick me up and send me back. I went to the Captain of the ship and he told me he had a stowaway.

He maneuvered the ship completely around, lowered the monkey ladder over the side and made the man get off into the water. I didn't know if he could swim or not, but I hope so because he was 300 to 400 yards from the pier.

In any event, we steamed out and headed again for the USA. Some twenty-one days later, we arrived at Patrick Henry. We were processed and sent to San Antonio to be discharged.

My most enduring memory of that voyage from Bari, Italy, was the very end of it. Everyone wanted to take a shower. A lot of the men took their uniforms off. I took off everything I had on and for all I know my clothes may be sitting in a pile in that shower stall to this day. I never looked back. I finished my shower, put on fresh clothes, flew to San Antonio and the next day went through the final processing, in a large room that had probably fifty typewriters, with a clerk behind each one.

The last man we talked with was a West Point colonel, whose job was to get people to accept a commission in the reserves. As it turned out, he had never been overseas. A friend of mine was sitting in a chair across from the colonel, who extolled the virtues of a reserve commission. I was not very attentive.

When he turned in my direction, I told him I did not care to participate. He made a reference that I felt impugned my patriotism and I got hot, instant, boiling hot. I said, "Sir, may I ask you a question?"

He replied that I could.

I asked if he were a West Point man? He replied that he was. I asked if he had been overseas? He asked me what that had to do with anything, but, no, he had not.

I said that I could understand from his answers how he felt because he had been subjected to military training, while my training was in the law, not in violence. I told him I had served my time in a theater overseas and was ready to go home. Everyone had stopped typing. I said unless he could give me a military order, I would not sign that paper. I just wanted to go home. He looked as if he wanted to have me shot, but he signed my discharge. I walked out of there and with a friend headed for the nearest beer joint and had a couple of beers.

Put it this way: It had taken a war to get me out of Houston and away from my law practice . . . and it would take another war to keep me away, and I was going to start it.

Section V

Fifty Years at Law
September 1945 — 1995

Chapter 5

One Good Case
Deserves Another

IN MY LIFETIME I have spent thousands of hours inside a courtroom. And for each of those hours, I have spent ten preparing my cases, and of these up to five trying to keep my client out of court.

The first duty of a client is to tell the truth, the entire truth, as he or she may best recall it. The second duty is to heed the advice of the attorney who is being paid to provide it.

There are few locations more austere or less accomodating than a courtroom. From the judge peering down from a chair like a throne, to the jury box and the witness stand, the tables for the opposing legal teams and the rows provided for the gallery, every inch of wood cries out: serious work is being done here; you are not meant to be comfortable. There are no furnishings, no relief for the eye save the occasional judicial portrait and the state or federal seal.

I have allowed myself a measure of license in the

selection of cases I chose to describe in these pages. I have settled upon a few that provide what I hope is a fair mix of drama, conflict and high financial stakes. I feel no pressure to impose upon the reader the details of the many cases that might reflect the lawyer's art, but in the end were of interest primarily to my client or me.

It would be like going to the theater, and having the producer describe the construction of the stage and backdrops, while the audience wants only to get on with the play. After I returned from the war, I was pleased to find a growing demand for my services. I was once again a volume dealer, taking personal injury cases that the large firms often didn't want. I cared about my clients — I think my record reflects that. I told them if I took their case not to lie to me! But I did not adopt them or take them to raise. I made a promise to myself: I would not fall in love with my cases. My philosophy was to try them, win them and move on to the next. I kept that promise. I have rarely looked back — until now.

I returned to Houston in late January of 1946 and soon had my office close to the courthouse and began to start my practice with the help of Earl Cox and others. But the major changes in my life were personal. I was married when I went into the service, and remained so throughout the conflict. But shortly after my homecoming we were divorced. There is nothing else that needs to be said about that experience. It was one of many marriages not strong enough to withstand the strain and long absence of war.

But it was the right decision, and a timely one, because it allowed me to meet the woman who would become my partner for the rest of my life. Mabel Roberson was the niece of Ruth Laws, who was the executive secretary of the Houston Bar Association. I was in her office one day when Mabel was visiting her aunt, and Mrs. Laws introduced us. I cannot be accused of wasting time; I invited Mabel to join me at a wedding reception for a lawyer, and we had our first date that night.

In an old-fashioned phrase, we were smitten. We began to see each other steadily and married within a year or so, on June 16, 1947. Mabel had a young daughter, Judy, from a previous marriage, and I loved her as my own. Judge Ewing Boyd, a friend to both of us, performed the service. Camille Berman, who was then working for Max Manuel at the Peacock Restaurant, on Fannin, across from the Texas State Hotel, prepared our wedding dinner. (Later, Camille opened and owned Maxim's, one of Houston's most elegant restaurants.) We went to New Orleans for our honeymoon.

The new Mrs. Parks was the daughter of Sam and Alta Roberson, of Angleton, a quiet town some 45 miles south of Houston. Her father was a cattleman, who owned the bank, the feed store, a day school, considerable land and much of what else there was in Brazoria County.

Her grandfather, on her father's side, ran for the U.S. Senate and lost and had little to show for it except a high stack of bills. The family had to sell off some of its land for twenty-five cents an acre to pay his debts. When her parents died, their home in Angleton became the property of the city, which turned it into a funeral home. For this, and other reasons, Mabel had little regard for politics.

But she knew and liked the legal profession. She was the grandaughter, on her mother's side, of a lawyer, who was for a period of time the district attorney in Portland, Oregon.

At this point, in the interest of fairness and modesty, I should allow Mabel Parks to testify for herself:

"When I met Fred he was just returning to his law practice. He was very nice looking, tall and vigorous. I was glad he was a lawyer, but several people had talked to him about the idea of his running for office. I told him if he got into politics, I would wish him well and say good-by. There would be no politics in my life. It is a necessary evil, as far as I'm concerned. That was the end of it.

"I knew the first rule for a lawyer's wife was not to interfere. He wasn't the kind of man who came home and talked about what happened that day at the office. But he would, on occasion, mention that he had accepted a lawsuit involving certain people, and did I know any of them? I was active in several charitable organizations, especially the Texas Children's Hospital, and in this work you met various people in the community. Fred did trust my judgment.

"When we married, I was a secretary for the Humble Oil and Refining Company, later Exxon, and he made me quit. After that, my interest was in helping him reach his goal — to be a great lawyer — in the best way I knew how, by giving him the solitude he needed when he was involved in an important case. Many nights he didn't go to bed, and I would keep the house quiet and not let the phone interrupt him. We have been married nearly fifty years and I never set foot in a courthouse to watch him try a case. I was afraid I might distract him."

To have a successful career in law involves many factors. But it helps to have a fair and impartial judge, a keen memory, a fresh shirt and an understanding wife.

The Houston I came home to in 1946 was a city that had tripled in size since my first arrival as a student. The Ship Channel now rated among the top three ports in the nation in tonnage. Houston was a rail and shipping center. Great fortunes were being made in oil. Texas was growing in political clout; John Nance Garner, from Uvalde, had served a term as vice-president under Franklin Roosevelt; Sam Rayburn exercised enormous influence as Speaker of the House, and Lyndon Johnson was making a move to run for the Senate. All of this combined to create new businesses, and a need for law firms and lawyers.

This was also a time when we believed in our symbols and stereotypes. All judges looked like Andy Hardy's father, played in the movie by the white-haired Harlan Stone. The phrase that measured great wealth was "rich as Rockefeller." Al Capone was to crime what Albert Einstein was to smartness. Reporters were hard-drinking, wise-cracking characters who stuck press cards in their hatbands.

And lawyers chased ambulances, and not just in the movies.

In truth, we were not far removed from that era in Houston, in the late 1940s and '50s. One aspect of this was the use of "runners," hustlers who solicited business for lawyers in return for a fee or kickback. This was a practice I fought against and had a hand in eventually getting rid of it.

The running of cases was a way of illegally obtaining employment in personal injury cases, by paying off the so-called runner, who would bring or send the client to the attorney's office. One effective method was to have an investigator with a two-way radio, who picked up police calls and went to the scene of the accident, taking the names of the insured people as well as witnesses. He would determine where these people lived, call upon them, tell them which lawyer or firm was the best to handle their case. In some instances, they would get them to sign a power of attorney and notify the firm that it had a new client.

The slickest operator in town was an individual who would get to the scene of, say, a bus accident, mingle with the crowd and finally would be included as a passenger on the bus. He would then, in turn, go to the hospital, cozy up to the injured and tell them which attorney they should hire. His fee would be a percentage of the recovery on the case. Example: if it settled for $1,000, the lawyer would keep $500 as his legal fee and then pay 25 percent ($125) to the runner.

The issue became so odorous that Earl Cox and I drafted a letter to be sent to both the members of the bar and the police department. Cox was considered the top personal injury attorney in that era. He had passed the bar at 21, without ever attending college. Earl didn't solicit cases, they came to him. Sadly, he died of a heart attack at the age of 50.

The letter would have required the police department, after investigating an accident, to write the insured parties and advise them to report the name, and license number of the car, of any attorney trying to solicit their case. Albert Jones, formally with Baker & Botts, killed that resolution in the Bar Association, although he later denied that he had anything to do with it. I felt the letter would have been a deterrent.

Example: I sued the Halliburton Company in a case that made a substantial recovery. I was called in when one of their key men had been severely injured, as he was being lifted from the boat to the deck of an offshore platform. The man operating the crane had actually pulled the load up (at that time, the men had to cling to a cable on the outside of the scoop.) This crewman fell some sixteen to eighteen feet and landed feet first on a steel deck. He was totally disabled. Halliburton was self-insured, and one of their managers had talked to him. The injured man said he wanted an attorney. When I was contacted by Halliburton, I told them to have him call me.

I think it spoke volumes for this large company, usually a defendant, to refer an insured employee to a personal injury attorney such as myself. He was a long and valued employee and they wanted him to have a fair compensation for his injuries.

He did and said he would like to send his brother to my office first to meet me. He was just being cautious. The brother invited me to the man's home in Port Arthur, the scene of the accident. After our visit, he asked me to handle the case. Then he showed me business cards from thirty-five lawyers who solicited his case from the day he was hospitalized until he returned home. I wish I had kept a copy of the list. Some were the "outstanding" plaintiff attorneys of the time.

As a result of this accident, the workers were no longer transported in this manner to the deck of an offshore platform. From then on, they were lifted in an enclosed cage.

Another example of mass running resulted when two tankers collided in the Gulf of Mexico, near New Orleans, both owned by Standard Oil Company. Several men were killed, badly injured or drowned. Who should step off one of the tankers but one of the most prominent attorneys in Houston, with Mandell & Wright, a firm that specialized in admiralty law. I later landed one case when the lady friend of a doctor I knew referred a woman to me whose husband had been killed, and who had been offered a settlement that seemed insufficient.

I took her case and told her I would only charge her a 50 percent fee of whatever we negotiated over and above what the insurance company was now offering. The insurers were anxious to talk settlement. I told them I had the strongest case of any because this particular seaman had the largest number of dependents. I asked for the maximum they paid Mandell and Wright, and told them to add $20,000 to it and I would settle, which we did.

The lady came to me later and said she had so many relatives, who were already circling her, and she wanted my help in keeping their hands off her money. At my suggestion, she bought a half-block of property in the Heights with a house and a condo on it, and had the whole area fenced in for her kids. I invested the money for her, opened a bank account for her, and did not charge a dime.

About ten years later, she called me and said she had a problem with her oldest son. He had broken into the courthouse, of all places, in another county, managed to get into the judge's chamber and slashed his leather chair with a pocket knife. I made an appointment with the judge and drove over to see him, having taken the liberty of having a new leather chair delivered to his court. I said hello and he asked me about the chair. I explained the circumstances: the death of the woman's husband and the hard time she had raising her children. I asked the judge to scare the boy half to death, but not to put him in jail. The lad got off.

I was vice president of the Texas Bar Association in 1957, and the running had gotten out of control. Members of the Galveston Bar filed a complaint that the Houston lawyers were running cases so openly, they could not make a living. The president of the Bar asked me to take care of it. I took their report and then talked to the insurance companies, who also had appealed for some sort of action.

There were two ongoing investigations, one into the conduct of Mandell & Wright, the other involving the Bates Brothers, who were nephews of Colonel

Bates, one of the powers at Fulbright Crooker. The Grievance Committee appealed to the Federal Court for relief for Mandell & Wright. Judge Haney entered an order requiring Mandell & Wright to withdraw in every case they had in the Southern District of Texas. A conservative estimate would place their loss in excess of $1 million. They could not refer the cases. It was a devastating blow, in image as much as monetary. Law firms cringe at the idea of being accused of an impropriety.

Arthur Mandell told Judge Haney that the order had been entered, they were found guilty and would take their punishment. But in a bitter aside, he offered to wager that no penalty would be levied against the Bates Brothers, who were just as guilty.

With that, Judge Haney called me into his chambers and asked me what I planned to do about the Bates Brothers. I told him their case was now before the Grievance Committee and I thought appropriate action would be taken. He repeated what Mandell had said. The investigation took on a new energy.

A meeting was scheduled for the Board of Directors in Galveston and one of the items on the agenda was whether or not the State Bar would advance funds (around $500) to the Court Reporter for transcribing the hearing against the Bates Brothers. I was in trial when the president of the Galveston Bar called and said, "I want to be sure that you attend this meeting and speak on this matter." I asked him to let everyone else talk, and to hold the meeting open until I could get there—around 7:00 P.M. I wanted the closing argument, which would not only allow me a certain dramatic weight, but solved the practical problem of driving from Houston to Galveston in time to address the board.

Several attorneys made their pitches. Opposing the motion were John Hill, Jim Kronzer, Newton Gresham and others who tried to minimize the issue, and did not want to embarrass Fulbright Crooker. I arrived, and concluded the hearings by repeating what Judge Haney had told me. I reviewed the sanctions taken against Mandell & Wright and said we should expect equal treatment for everyone. The motion cleared by one vote — mine. The Bar advanced the money and the Bates brothers were disciplined and in time split up. One later became a state district judge.

There is not a sliver of doubt in my mind that my role in this action cost me the presidency of the state bar. A letter from Fulbright Crooker went to attorneys all over the state, asking them not to vote for me. (A Dallas firm had waged a similar campaign against Henry Strasburger.) You do not gain this sort of prestige position by offending the large law firms.

DEATH BY BLOWOUT

In 1962, a young geologist, on his first job in West Texas, finished his day shift, got in his car to go home and ran into a cloud of gas contaminated by a wild well blowing out. The wind blew the natural gas over the road and ignited his car. He jumped out, climbed over a fence and threw himself on the ground to smother the flames which engulfed his body.

I was retained to take the case. I went out to West Texas, where the well was, and later filed suit in Houston against the contractor and also against the manufacturer of the blowout preventor. The well burned for more than twenty days before Red Adair and his fire fighters could put it out. They recorded this battle on film, and the crew got so close in taking the pictures that when they stopped shooting the extreme heat melted the camera equipment.

The people from the blowout well were standing near the road when a car went by with one person in it. He proceeded on to a point where there was sufficient gas on the road; his car ignited and he jumped out of his car on fire, climbed a barbed wire fence and fell. They had rushed to him and, as I was asking questions of these men in a deposition, the only sound you could hear was the scratching of the court reporter's pen. I asked: "Was he conscious?" Yes. "Did he say anything?" Yes. I said, "Repeat to me what he said." The response was: "Dear God, don't let this happen to me because of my children." He was twenty-six years old. He died in agony.

I had subpoenas served on the workers from all of the shifts, and I hired an old well digger to advise me on the case. He told me the proper procedure was that the driller should have closed the blowout preventor. In case it did not work, the safest place to go was to get beneath the rig floor. By continuing the questioning, it would be determined that the blowout preventor had never been put on the well.

The heat from the fire had frozen the machinery

and it was still open. This equipment was moved from the site to Houston after the fire and stored for testing.

At the start of the second depositions, Larry Morris, the attorney for the defendants, took the position that I could not make the connection that the blowout preventor was the same one that was at the well. I accepted the challenge. I said, okay, I can provide that connection and before the case is over your client will pay for it.

I contacted the highest ranking official with the company and asked him if the blowout preventor came off his well. I also advised him that if he wouldn't answer my questions, I might have to take depositions from everyone in his office, and he would have me underfoot for ten days or two weeks. He talked to Larry Morris and convinced him to make that stipulation — that it was the same blowout preventor — and we continued with the depositions.

We were ready to try the case and it was assigned to trial. On the morning of the trial, an attorney who worked with Morris appeared and said Morris was sick and could not proceed. I told the Court I had been expecting something of this nature and had my doubts that he was so ill that he could not conduct the defense. I asked the Court to give me about thirty minutes and I would take testimony from this attorney and see what developed.

I asked the new attorney for the name of Morris' doctor. He told me, and I asked the Court if I could use the phone and call the doctor. I could not get the doctor to voluntarily come to court, so I sent an associate of mine to get a subpoena. We then put the doctor on the stand and I took his testimony. It developed that Morris had a post nasal drip and had it for years. The court reset the trial for the next day.

The other side (with the approval of the absent Mr. Morris) decided they would try to settle the case. They invited me to lunch in one of their rooms at the Rice Hotel. We began drinking and I knew they would try to get me drunk so I would settle the case for less money. Every time we had a round, I would go up on the settlement price. They were getting drunk and finally decided to adjourn to the bathroom to discuss the situation, but I could overhear what they were saying: "This s.o.b. is raising his price every time we make an offer. We're not getting anywhere."

When they came back into the room, they decided we would settle the case. The blowout preventor had not been installed, so a handsome settlement was reached.

Larry Morris was a great compensation attorney. He would make a good case for his client, asking high compensation, and then reduce it down to where it seemed almost insignificant. I had heard stories about his arguments and had some of them transcribed. I then began to pick up on what he was doing.

In the argument, the plaintiff would open, then the defense would give its argument and the plaintiff would close. Morris would say they were willing to pay whatever they were told they owed for damages, and were prepared to pay right then. In my closing argument, I told the jury I had prepared a check payable to my client, and I quoted the argument made by Mr. Morris. I said, if he would waive any motion for a new trial or right of appeal and, furthermore, if he would waive the obligation of the jury to answer the charge of the court, and be bound by the amount of money they awarded, then please sign the check and whatever amount the jury wrote in was the amount the company would pay this man for his injuries.

Larry did get up and tell the jury that he meant what he said and was not trying to deceive them. The jury gave me more by far than the judgment we felt we would receive — $201,000.

While I was handling this case, I was approached by an attorney from West Texas who said he understood I had been employed in the above lawsuit and had done considerable investigation. He said he represented the landowners in the area of the blowout, and because of the length of time the well burned, considerable gas was lost and it had cost those with a mineral interest quite a lot of money in lost revenues.

He asked me if I would talk to the mineral owners and schedule a meeting. I went over to his office and the landowners all showed up driving late model Cadillacs. I made my presentation and pointed out where millions of dollars had been lost, but they refused to hire anyone. I had experts look at the oil and gas reserves and got a preliminary opinion as to how much oil and gas had been lost.

They were afraid if they sued, there would be reprisals from the oil companies and they did not want to lose their revenue checks, and possibly their Cadillacs.

DEATH BY MISFIRE

In April of 1961, a B-52 bomber was on a routine training exercise over New Mexico to teach the potential gunners to shoot down enemy planes. In this case, the supposed enemy aircraft was the B-52 with a full crew of American airmen.

A jet fighter-interceptor was making a series of simulated attack passes at the bomber. The procedure was for the gunner to get the plane in his sights, lock on, and pull the trigger. In actual combat, this would fire sidewinder missiles which would destroy the enemy. For this exercise, it should have snapped a picture to see if the sighting was on target.

Something went tragically wrong. When the gunner pulled the trigger, ostensibly to take a photograph, the missile fired and blew the B-52 out of the sky, killing the two pilots, a navigator and disabling and disfiguring two crewmen. The navigator, Captain Stephen Carter, was married to a Houston woman, who became my initial client. Charlotte Carter's third child, a son, was born eleven days after his father's death.

It was the hardest kind of destruction to accept. This wasn't combat. This wasn't in wartime, in Europe or the Middle East or any of the world's trouble spots. It happened over New Mexico, on a peaceful April day, with American weapons killing American boys.

When I got the case, I analyzed it this way: For

the missile to accidentally discharge, instead of taking a picture, there had to be a defective part in the weaponry. If there was a defective part, there had to be a corrected part to make it perform the way it should. I sent an investigator out and told him what I thought, and that he was not to come back without the defective part and the modified part. I also told him I didn't care how he got it — not to tell me — just get it. He went to a base in New Mexico and came back about thirty days later.

I represented a few of the survivors of the families and filed a lawsuit. Bill Harvin of Baker & Botts represented the insurance company and I notified him that I wanted to take depositions. He said he wanted to talk to me. He said he had advised the insurance people that I knew what I was doing, that I would make a thorough discovery and knew how to try the case.

He also said he had asked them if they would take the estimate of what it would cost to prepare for trial, and add that amount to a settlement, so we would not have to try the case. I told Harvin that would be fine with me.

(To understand this, keep in mind that insurance companies don't take big risks, so they have high risk insurance and only the insurance companies can be stockholders. They make up 100 percent of the stockholders and act as a separate insurance carrier. All of these catastrophic insurance claims are covered by these re-insurance companies.)

I made individual brochures on each client I had

before talking settlement. A lot of the people apparently did not realize any insurance was involved. They were Arizona National Guardsmen and the story got out that one of them had an attorney; then all the others wanted me to represent them, also.

I was suing the manufacturer of the modified fighter plane and the manufacturer of the sidewinder missile equipment.

We made an appointment and the conference would be held in New York. Mrs. Parks and I flew to New York and checked into the Carlyle Hotel. Bill took us out the night before the meeting to the Rainbow Room in Rockefeller Center.

The offices of the insurance company were very plain, with uncomfortable furniture. There were no cushions on the chairs, no magazines to read. Here came a little, bandy-legged Irishman with a twinkle in his eye. He was the head of claims — the company dealt in the billions of dollars — and after the usual amenities I told him I understood that they wanted to discuss a settlement.

I told him I had made an investigation as to the cause of this accident and, as a result, it developed there was a defective part and a modified part to fix the problem. I reached in my briefcase and pulled out both parts.

For the purpose of discussion, he said, they would admit liability. I told him liability had two facets: negligence and how much. The parts established negligence, now how much were these cases worth? We had established liability.

We went through the dead and disabled cases —
case by case, and I gave him the amount of my demand. He said it was more than he was authorized to
expend and he would have to submit the case to a
committee. He said the committee meets every day
and he would present it to them in the morning. I
asked him if he would recommend accepting the figure, when it was submitted. He said, yes. I asked him if
he had ever recommended a settlement that had been
turned down. He said, no.

I told him I would be in my suite at the Carlyle
Hotel and would wait to hear from him. The next
morning, about 11:00 A.M., the head of the claims department called and said he had the authority to settle
the case at my figure, but there was a hitch. They all
had to be settled collectively. I agreed, and said that I
would furnish him a breakdown on each case, but we
must exchange the check and the releases at the same
time. When I settled with the clients, I wanted to
make only one trip. I told him that he could check
with Bill Harvin; my word was my bond. I wouldn't
negotiate any of the checks until he had all of the
signed releases in his custody.

I figured out the amounts and told my young associate to settle them. He was reluctant to go. They
were too important, he said, to handle by himself.
That, I explained, was why I wanted him to be the one
on the road. If he ran into a problem he could call me
and I'd have time to think about how to solve it. If I
went out, I had no way to pass the buck or buy time.

The associate called one day and said he was in

Los Angeles, and the lady he was trying to settle with had engaged another attorney. I asked if she had told him that? He said, yes, she had not signed the release and as it happened, he was calling from the attorney's office. I asked if he realized she already had an attorney? With that, he handed him the phone.

I said to the so-called new attorney: "Look, you s.o.b. I will tell you what you are going to do. You will call your client in and have her sign the release and endorse the check and give it to my man. Also, tell her she does not owe you any money."

He asked what I would do if he refused. I told him I would go to Los Angeles on the next plane and stay there until I had him disbarred. I told him I had recorded the telephone conversation and a copy would go to the Grievance Committee. She signed the release and endorsed the check. My associate called me after he got back to his hotel. I told him to come on home. All the cases had been settled. The settlements came to one million, two hundred seventy-five thousand dollars, a record sum at the time, for a case that not many knew could be tried.

MONEY BREEDS STRANGE BEDFELLOWS

On another occasion, I had been hired by Nathan Friedman to settle his father's interest in the Sands Hotel in Las Vegas when he died. This led to a friendly encounter with the noted jurist and banker, Judge Jim Elkins.

Nathan was the son of Jakie Friedman, a dapper,

With former President Ronald Reagan, in the Oval Office.

A night on the town with Mrs. Parks and Henry Kissinger.

There have been few first ladies as popular as Barbara Bush.

With longtime friends, former President George Bush and Barbara.

Giving advice to Senator Phil Gramm.

My tablemate is James Baker, former Secretary of State.

I'm all ears listening to Jack Nicklaus, who designated the course at Lochinvar.

Showing Nicklaus how to keep the clubhead straight.

ХВОСТОВАЯ
ЧАСТЬ
ФЮЗЕЛЯЖА

TAIL PART OF
THE FUSELAGE

On visit to Moscow, saw what was left of U-2 spy plane.

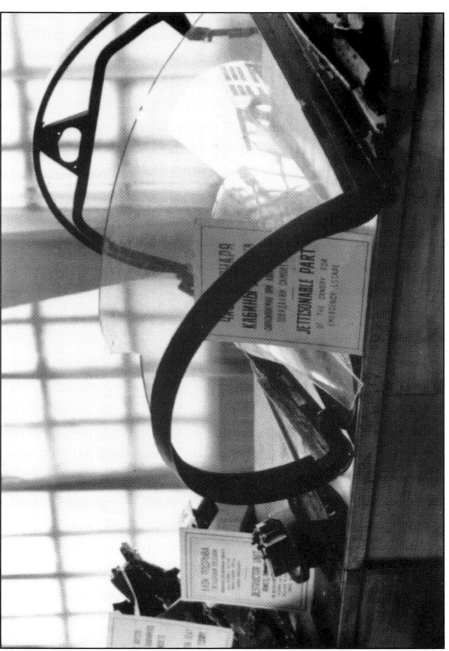

Top of U-2's cockpit, jettisoned by pilot, was nearly intact.

Scroll from Chinese friends offers "Heavenly Blessings" on 87th birthday, 1993

The bronze star, awarded 1945.

Fred Parks and H. E. "Pete" Carrico,
Induction dinner of Confrerie de la
Chaine Des Rotisseurs, October 29,
1978, wine cellar of Petroleum Club.

*Exchanging toasts with Pete Carrico in wine cellar of the Petroleum Club, at
d'Escoffier induction dinner.*

Bombs away from Black 'N' on routine bombing mission in northern Italy.

Debris falling from Black 'N' which has been struck by flack.

Flack burst from one 3-gun battery

Black 'N' on fire flying almost upside down. Later crashed — no survivors

Fred and Mrs. Parks at Leisure.

With d'Escoffier medal and mini-rose in lapel. (photo by David Postma.)

colorful, sawed-off character who was partial to flashy cowboy suits and glittering gold jewelry. Jakie had owned a gambling house at the end of Main Street in Houston, until the Texas Rangers shut him down. He moved to Las Vegas, where he owned a twenty-five percent interest in the Sands Hotel and Casino at the time of his death.

Nathan asked me to go to Las Vegas to look after his father's holdings. He said he wanted to keep as much of the Sands investment as he could, but it was negotiable. Whatever I could get, he would give me half as my fee.

I got a very quick education in big time gambling. The books showed that Jakie had gambled away all of his ownership. There was an attorney representing the Sands and other casinos — and, I suspected, the Mafia. I had an accountant look at the books. Based upon the figures we were shown, he reported that Mr. Friedman had nothing. I told Nathan to settle for whatever he could.

The Sands said they would take care of Jakie's widow for as long as she lived. She moved into the hotel, had an unlimited power to sign vouchers for cash, was provided a chauffeur and car. They arranged a job for Nathan at another casino, as the collector of delinquent accounts in Houston.

The interesting part of the situation was that Nathan had said, "See if you can settle for some interest in the Sands and I will give you a percentage of what I get." I asked Nathan where the money was going to come from. At that time, a point of ownership, which was one percent, was selling for $40,000.

I already knew the answer. I talked to Judge Elkins, knowing of his close relationship with Jakie. I explained what Nathan wanted. He said to tell Nathan that if he needed to buy one percent or ten percent, he could draft on his bank, known today as Texas Commerce, and the money would be forthcoming.

As a prelude to that conversation, I should mention the reason why the gambler and the judge were such good friends. At one time, so the story went, the Elkins' bank was in trouble. He called Jakie, a big depositor who dealt in large amounts of cash. Elkins told Jakie the bank was in danger of being closed. The Big Little Man asked how much he needed to tide him over, then made the deposit. They enjoyed each other, taking trips to the Kentucky Derby and other lively locations.

I later represented Nathan during his divorce, while his wife retained Percy Foreman. I wanted to keep the matter clean and simple, stating the terms as "one dollar and other considerations." As a gambler, Nathan dealt almost entirely in cash. He had agreed to pay her, in cash, $30,000 a year for five years. We had agreed on the settlement eight months earlier. All that remained was the schedule of payments.

Still, for months, Percy would not allow her to be served so we could begin the proceedings. He kept her confined to her house. When my patience ran out, I had my secretrary call Mrs. Friedman and tell her that her daughter, Carolyn, had been in an accident and was on the way to the hospital. When she bolted out the door, the process server handed her the subpoena.

(The daughter would become well known in charitable circles by her married name, Carolyn Farb.)

Foreman was outraged. "Goddamn you," his voice thundered over the telephone line, "how could you pull a trick like that?"

I said, "Well, sir, Percy, I took a page out of your book."

Percy wanted drama and a contested filing. He warned me that Mrs. Friedman had a gun and was threatening to kill Nathan in the courtroom. Given the agitated mental state so common to the breakup of any marriage, I did not dismiss the warning.

On the day of the hearing, contrary to the canon of judicial ethics, I led her into a private room and said, "You've known me a long time and I've never lied to you. I hear you have a gun and if Nathan takes the stand you plan to kill him. But let me say this: if you have a gun and you use it the first person you need to shoot is Percy, because the money you're going to get is the same today as it was eight months ago."

It wasn't pleasant, divorces never are, but we got it done.

DON'T LET THE STARS GET IN YOUR EYES

When you have dealt with matters of life and death, with the fates of widows and workmen maimed on their jobs, a touch of glamor might seem a welcome change of pace. But anytime you see a sentence that includes the words "beautiful," "Hollywood" and "divorce," the wise lawyer should carefully rethink his values.

Such cases are certain to generate a number of headlines, but they are often in direct proportion to the size of the headaches.

In the spring and summer of 1961, the actress Hedy Lamarr wanted to reopen and amend the terms of her property settlement from Howard Lee, on the grounds that he had concealed additional assets from her. Lee, a Houston oilman, and Lamarr had divorced a year earlier. Hedy had received cash, oil leases and securities.

Lee had since married another actress, Gene Tierney, which had to be one of the more impressive parlays in Hollywood's long and colorful marital history.

Let me say at the outset that I did not want to take this case. But I owed a favor to Jerry Geisler, a Los Angeles attorney who represented many of the major stars of that time. He called and asked if I would act as Hedy's counsel in Houston. I told him, no, but he said he was calling in his markers — that I owed him one. I finally agreed.

Howard Lee, who was from a pioneer Texas oil family and distantly related to Robert E. Lee, was represented by a friend of mine, Lewis Dickson. Howard was a cordial man who did not deserve the grief that he bought with his heart.

I undertook the case with few illusions. No one could control Hedy. She was born in Hungary, growing up as Hedwig Eva Maria Kiesler. She legally changed her named to Hedy Lamarr in 1941. She had been discovered as a teen ager in Berlin by the director Max Reinhardt, and first came to wide public notice in a movie called "Ecstasy," in which she appeared nude for a brief scene running through a sylvan glade. This was considered shocking by the standards of the day, but did not seem to hurt Hedy's career. It was rumored for years that the young girl pictured naked, from the back, on the label of a spring water was, in fact, Hedy Lamarr. I don't believe it was ever established one way or another, but the sales of the beverage soared.

She later co-starred with such actors as Charles Boyer, Clark Gable, Spencer Tracy, James Stewart, Walter Pidgeon and William Powell.

I told Geisler to tell Hedy to get on a plane under an assumed name; to check into a hotel, also under an assumed name, and to call me when she arrived in town. I specifically said I did not want any publicity. He said, fine.

A week went by, and I picked up the *Houston Press* one afternoon and there it was, a headline that screamed the news: "HEDY LAMARR ARRIVES IN HOUSTON." According to the story, she was met at the airport by a doctor friend of hers and was whisked off. I waited four or five days — no phone call, no Hedy. Finally, I drove to the doctor's home and he came to the door. I asked him if I could speak to Hedy and he said she wasn't there. I told him he was lying.

As our voices rose, here came Hedy in a "painting smock." She had been painting, one of her amusements.

I told her she had better come to see me at my office or she could wind up in contempt of court and land in jail. She reacted calmly. Hedy had gotten into trouble with the court before I represented her by sending her maid to the court and saying she was unable to attend whenever she received a subpoena.

Hedy's suit against Howard Lee was weak. But there was another, more interesting story lurking in the wings. When she was still underage, one of the richest men in the world, Fritz Mandl, fell in love with her. He persisted, followed her to London, took her to his home in Switzerland, and eventually married her. She later went to Hollywood.

The man was a Catholic and she subsequently got a divorce in Mexico and then married Howard Lee. When Lee filed for divorce, Hedy's attorneys could not produce evidence that she had ever been divorced from her first husband. So we had to prove her marriage to Lee was, in fact, legal.

At that time, I was reasonably well known over the state because I lectured in different cities in Texas. I went to El Paso and contacted a friend who had a law practice there, dealing extensively in Mexico. I told him I knew that Hedy Lamarr had been married and divorced and that I believed she had been divorced in Juarez. I told him to find the divorce decree. Eventually, the document was found. It had been filed in the wrong year, but it was a legitimate divorce decree.

Armed with that information, I felt better. Mr. Mandl's attorneys contacted me (he had several attorneys, along with homes or estates in Germany, Paris, London, New york and businesses in South America.) They offered me a really indecent amount of money if

Hedy would sign some papers which would, in the eyes of the Catholic church, invalidate the marriage. I tried talking her into signing the papers to annul the marriage, but she refused, for reasons she never cared to explain.

Eventually, the Lee case was settled with modest improvements for Hedy. But I have memories of an interesting night, when Mrs. Parks and I entertained Hedy at my club in Palm Desert, California, the El Dorado Country Club. While we waited, I asked Mabel what she thought Hedy would be wearing, because in those days "dinner at the club" meant the women wore their finest jewelry and fashions. There was an orchestra and a dance floor.

Hedy arrived at the club wearing a kerchief over her head and was not dressed for the "evening," as the other women were. Still, nothing could obscure the fact that she was a beautiful woman. We sat near the dance floor. Soon the wine steward and Hedy were good friends, having discovered that they came from the same little town in Hungary. We were the only people in the club who got any service that night.

Finally, after trying to talk Hedy into signing an annulment to her first marriage, I surrendered. Had she signed the papers, taken the money he offered and invested it, she could have lived comfortably, even lavishly, the rest of her life. Money was no object to the man. I read sadly in later years of incidents where Hedy was arrested for shoplifting.

I had to accept my defeat. This was the first client that I could not convince, or even reason with, in my entire career.

MEDICINE AND THE COURTS

When I first began the practice of law at the offices of Burris & Benton, the scientific tools were primitive as compared with today. Medical experts were few and far between. I have tried cases, as I look back, that I should never have tried. I did so based on chiropractic and osteopath reports, verified by X-rays, some of which were so opaque you could not see the skeleton. Little by little, X-rays were improved. We followed these improvements closely.

Dr. Peyton Denman originally was a doctor for timber companies up in East Texas and had been effective later as a witness in their cases. He came to Houston and in keeping with his experience and background, was employed by insurance companies to testify in personal injury cases. In due course, the companies attempted to make him reduce his fees because, in their opinion, he was making too much money. He told them he would not reduce his fees and, furthermore, he would not represent any of them in the future. Then he wrote a letter to several plaintiff's attorneys, in turn giving his background and the reason he quit working for the insurance companies.

Burris & Benton employed him and he and I became good friends. He taught me a good deal about handling my cases. For example, if I knew on Friday that I had to go to trial on Monday, we would go by his office and look at all the X-rays and his reports. He would explain how he would testify and what he thought the opinion of the doctor for the other side would be. He kept current with the science of medicine and was instrumental in helping to educate me in this area.

One day, a prominent Houston physician and a close friend of mine, called and asked me to meet him at the River Oaks Country Club on my way home. We had a couple of drinks and he told me he had never felt more humiliated in his life. He was unsure what to do and needed advice. He had gone to the courthouse to testify in a case. The attorney had taken his records and, on cross examination, took his files and found a discrepancy in the doctor's testimony. He lost the case. He said, "What can I do?" I said it was simple.

I told him to make a thorough examination of his records, get his facts, dictate a report, and send the original to the insurance company and keep two or three copies in the file and destroy everything else. Then he would have only the written report to review, and that mistake would never happen again.

NORTHERN EXPOSURE

In 1958, a lawyer at Baker and Botts called me one day and said they had a case they could not handle and wondered if I would consider taking it. The case was in Alaska, which was still a territory at the time and not yet a state.

I reviewed the issues very carefully with the client and realized there was a critical problem of being able to file the suit in both Alaska and in Seattle to meet the deadline for the statute of limitations. I wrestled with whether to take the case or not, but finally decided I would.

As a precaution, I had the client sign a waiver, agreeing not to sue us if we were unable to meet the deadline.

I shut everything down in the office and we went to work and filed the suit. The filing was put on the last plane out of Seattle and we filed it there and in Fairbanks. The substance of the suit was as follows:

The United States government was building a secret installation called Ilson Air Force Base in Fairbanks. In order to keep the utilities from freezing, they dug a tunnel and placed all the utility lines inside. It was named the Utilidor Tunnel. The contractor finished all of his work and the tunnel in turn was accepted by the government.

The government experienced difficulty in the operation and rehired the superintendent, who had worked for the contractor, to correct them. They hired him on a certain basis.

A government agent went to the contractor and said they would like to hire his chief supervisor to straighten out the problems. Somehow, in spite of the government's time-honored reputation for paperwork, and its penchant for triplicate copies, all of this was done on a verbal basis.

The supervisor took on the job, and in the process of examining the systems they were having trouble with, he and two men were in the Utilidor Tunnel when a steam line broke. He pushed his two assistants out of the hole. However, when he tried to get out himself, unfortunately, the steam blinded him. He retained a little vision, but was diagnosed as industrially

162

blind, meaning he was incapable of continuing his work.

This was our lawsuit. I started to develop it as I developed all lawsuits. At the time, I was busy as well with other cases and hired a Ben Slider to take depositions for me, and offered him a piece of the recovery for his fee. His expenses and mine were to be deducted and he would have a percentage of the net fee.

I flew to Alaska and found the circumstances intriguing, to say the least. To begin with, you had a top secret base. You couldn't even get entry to it through any regular channels. A contractor and I got together and he put a hard hat on me and I walked in with his crew. There were signs posted that forbid anyone from taking photographs or reproducing any sites or equipment. But I had a good memory and when we got outside, I made my sketches.

One of the things I did was to hire Mike Stepovich, who later became the first appointed governor of Alaska, as my co-counsel. The government's attorney wore a pair of black and white spectator shoes that had never been cleaned, so they were almost all black. He owned a large dog that followed him in and out of the courtroom when he was trying a case.

We had several preliminary meetings and then a visit with the judge. At the conclusion of the hearing, the judge asked me, "Is there anything else?" I said, only partly in jest, "Your honor, I think you ought to take judicial notice that I am from Texas, my blood is thin and therefore this case should be set in the summertime." (Judicial notice is a recognition by the

163

court of a fact or ruling that has no dispute, such as the time the sun comes up or that Thanksgiving falls on a Thursday.)

He said he would see if he couldn't accommodate me. We finished with the depositions and got into the serious negotiations. They made a good faith settlement offer, which I rejected. At that time, Fred Collins, of my office, who is now deceased, and I wrote a memorandum saying that under no circumstances would we settle for the amount offered. I felt I could get substantially more money for my client.

In addition, I had a slightly ulterior motive. There was no time pressure. I planned to stop at Kodiak Island, where I had arranged to go hunting for a Kodiak bear, on the way back from Alaska after we settled the case.

Meanwhile, Mrs. Parks and I had scheduled a trip to Europe well in advance, and when we got home I learned, to my absolute shock, that the case had been settled. I raised hell with Collins, who said Slider had decided on his own that he would spring a surprise on Fred Parks and have the case settled by the time he returned from Europe. There was nothing I could do.

What Slider and his clerk did was get themselves a trip to Alaska and I missed out on my bear hunt.

Except for what turned out to be the sensitive nature of the suit, it could serve as a reminder that when you sometimes try to mix business with pleasure, it can backfire on you.

In due course, the checks came in to me and Slider, having signed the settlement papers, was a payee on the checks. I called and gave him hell for settling the case, but conceded there was nothing much I could do except send him his fee — once he documented his expenses.

In turn, he told me to send him an accounting of *my* expenses and then he would send me his, at which point we would then negotiate the check and disburse it.

That sort of infuriated me. I had enjoyed a pleasant relationship with Slider up until then, but for him to just take over my lawsuit and settle it while I was away and without my authority really burned me. I decided to teach him a lesson.

My client endorsed the check and I did the same, as well as endorsing it for Ben Slider, by Fred Parks, for deposit only, and put it in my bank. It took about ten days for the check to clear. I made part of the distributions and called Slider.

"Ben," I said, "I have been waiting for you to give me your expenses so that I can disburse the money." I told him, for his information, the checks had been negotiated and paid and I had the remainder of the cash. If he wanted his expenses, and his portion of the fee, he would have to send me his receipts right away. He asked me if I had endorsed his name on the check.

I told him I sure had. I could hear him sputter. He said he would go to the Grievance Committee of the Texas Bar Association and have me disbarred.

I asked him when he was planning to go. He said, right away. I told him I would meet him there and, while he was filing his complaint, I would file one stating that he had acted without my authority, had made

165

an unnecessary trip to Alaska, resulting in unjustified expenses, and that he had accepted a settlement that I deemed to be low and had previously turned down. I concluded by saying we would submit our grievances and see who got disbarred.

He backed down, sent me his accounting, and I promptly mailed a check for his fee plus expenses. That was the last time we ever communicated.

There was an interesting footnote to this suit. When the case was finished, my client returned to his home in Beaumont, where his wife had an excellent job. Of course, when he got back he had no employment and no prospects of any in his field, in view of his lost vision. He had sent all of his money home and his wife had socked it away in her bank account and had filed for divorce.

He came to see me and said he had nothing to live on. I asked if his wife was working and he said yes. I tried that case and won a decree in his favor. It was perhaps the first case ever decided in the state of Texas where the court ruled that a woman had to support her ex-husband.

THE MOODY BLUES

Estate cases, contesting a will, are among the most bitter known to law, often dividing families, turning brothers against sisters, children against their parents, maligning the dead and destroying reputations. On occasion no one wins.

In Texas, there was one case that surpassed all

others, and it involved the wills of Mr. and Mrs. William Lewis Moody, Jr., who died fourteen years apart.

For perhaps one hundred years, three or four families controlled the destiny of Galveston and foremost among these were the Moodys. I was driving in my car in July, of 1954, when I heard on the radio that W. L. Moody had died at the age of 89. Suffice it to say that until that moment, I had given little if any thought to the family or its vast holdings. At the time, he was considered one of the nation's ten wealthiest and least known men. His life contradicted the most of the popular cliches about free-spending Texas millionaires.

He was never an oilman, although his business empire took in nearly everything else in the state: real estate, cotton, thirty hotels, three banks, eleven ranches, two newspapers, a printing plant and what was then the largest insurance company (American National) west of the Mississippi River.

Although he neither smoked, drank nor played cards for money, he did not object if others did. In his heyday, the island had become the gambling mecca of Texas, as well as the state's only city with open saloons. Moody welcomed the tourists that gambling brought to his hotels.

His sharp bargaining led to many disagreements, including one with his only living son, whose spending habits he disapproved. After a falling out in 1950, he never again spoke in the presence of his son. In the will, William L. Moody III received the sum of one dollar.

One day out of the blue, I got a call from an attorney named Carl Wright Johnson in San Antonio. I had met Carl during my activities on behalf of the state bar and we had been friends for several years. He told me that he and Pat Swearingen and Russell Markwell had been employed in a matter involving the Moody estate. They were coming to Houston to see me, and engage me to take depositions in the case. They represented the son, who had inherited one dollar.

(I assumed that it was because of my representation in the Texas City disaster that they wanted me to be part of their legal team.)

Before his death, the elder Moody put nearly all of his estate in a tax-exempt foundation. Executive control of his companies passed to his older daughter, Mrs. Mary Moody Northen, then sixty-one, who had been devoted to her father, whose frugal nature closely resembled her own. For many years, she lived in a house her father owned on the boulevard. He left it unfurnished, but when they had guests his workmen would move furniture out of one of his hotels. When the guests left, it was moved back to the hotel.

Mary Moody was dependent upon and totally loyal to her father, who never acknowledged her behavior as anything irregular. She refused to have electrical appliances in her home. She had no radio. Her house was heated by a wood burning stove. She dressed plainly, in styles popular twenty years earlier, and favored black cotton stockings. She wore her hair piled in a turn-of-the-century fashion. As late as 1953, she drove a 1928 Studebaker until her father heard that people were laughing at her. He then gave her a Cadillac.

As a child, according to friends, Mary Moody had no formal schooling. Now and then, private tutors taught her until she was sixteen. But she was said to be an avid reader of newspapers, in particular the want ads and property transactions. A widow at the time of her father's death, she moved into his mansion, three blocks from her own house. It had all the modern conveniences and a staff of servants.

I did some research and drove to Galveston. The will had a provision that if anyone contested it and failed, they would forfeit any bequests in their favor. In order to be able to prosecute this case, we would have to rely on the testimony of people who had bequests coming, and the obvious fear was that they would not jeopardize those by telling the truth.

The Moodys in Galveston were represented by the DeBrill law firm. The older brother was known as "Liver Lips." Based on my research, I came up with the idea of not filing a lawsuit, but filing instead a petition to *perpetuate testimony in contemplation* of filing a lawsuit, which was a device that simply preserved the evidence.

The Rules of Evidence were such that in some instances you had difficulty in getting a witness and exhibits together. If the exhibits were controlled by a different witness, then the witness you were questioning would know nothing about the exhibits.

In view of the provision that raised the risk of forfeit, some of the heirs declined to cooperate with us because the bank might interpret their action as contesting the will. I found a little used rule, 187 of the Rules of Civil Procedure, Volume 31, of the Texas Jurisprudence "Discovery" section. A Supreme Court case had upheld that a procedure to perpetuate testimony was not a contest, but merely protected the testimony for future use if you decided to file a contest.

I went to San Antonio and laid out the tactic to Carl Wright Johnson and he agreed to proceed that way. I prepared it and we filed the motion in Galveston.

Liver Lips DeBrille and his brother had hired ex-governor Dan Moody, a distant cousin of the deceased, as additional counsel. We were having dinner and drinks on the eve of the hearing, and I asked Mr. Swearingen, who was the former counsel for the Standard Oil Company, to define what he expected me to do the next day because that would determine whether I had a second drink or not.

The logical man to take the lead would have been Russell Markwell, but Swearingen told me to start the trial and see how it went. That night I went back to my hotel room and organized my work. I led off the next day and never relinquished the role as leading counsel until the litigation was over.

The case was moving along when it became necessary for Liver Lips DeBrille to furnish certain records. He left to go to his office to retrieve the documents and his brother stayed behind. We were standing around, waiting, and I grabbed Pat Swearingen and asked him, why don't we put Liver Lips' brother on the stand and prove how the will was drawn and signed? I had a strong hunch we would find a discrepancy.

My investigation had turned up an intriguing set of facts. The will of Mrs. Moody, who had been bedridden for more than a year, was drawn at the request of her husband. Two nurses signed as witnesses. Mrs. Moody's signature, written illegibly, appeared twice and was partially written a third time. She died six months later, on August 22, 1942. That same day the Moody Foundation was created with only Mary Moody Northen, among the children, named as a trustee.

I asked the judge if we could use this idle time to proceed with more testimony. He gave us his quick approval and we had the brother sworn in and put on the stand. I asked him and, in great detail, he explained what Mr. Moody wanted in the will. It had been drawn in accordance with those wishes and was prepared for signature and was reviewed for attesting by the witnesses. He said they all came to his brother's office and went through the formalities before Mr. Moody signed, followed by the witnesses.

I asked where they were seated and whose pen they used. I asked if they all signed with the same pen. He said, yes. I asked why, if they were all signed with the same pen, all the signatures were in black ink with the exception of one, which was signed with blue ink. About that time, Liver Lips walked in and screamed at his brother to get off the stand. He was extremely upset, to say the least, but we had the testimony and it was helpul.

When the trial re-convened, DeBrille offered affidavits of people which I regarded as not admissible, but Judge Hugh Gibson let them in, anyway. I asked him if, by the next day, I could introduce court affidavits and he said, yes.

When the court adjourned for the day, I called my secretary and dictated an affidavit and asked her to read it to a man I had interviewed in San Antonio. I put in a call to him and told him to catch a plane in Houston. Then I called a young attorney in my office, George Cire, who became a federal judge and is now deceased. I told George if the affidavit was correct to have the witness sign it; if it had to be changed he could write in the changes and initial them. But I knew it was substantially correct because I had taken it from his previous statements.

I instructed my secretary to be sure that George met me at a certain cafe in Galveston. I finished my lunch and was waiting impatiently, checking my watch, because the judge had ordered us to be back in court at 1:30 P.M. Cire arrived with a few minutes to spare. I looked at the affidavit, presented it to the judge and asked if he noticed that it countered every point the other side had made with their affidavits. Judge Gibson seemed to be waffling from his earlier position, which leaned in our favor and I said, politely, that it was time for him to either fish or cut bait.

The judge called a recess and as I walked across the room Dan Moody called me aside. He asked if I had seen the "holdover cage" in the courthouse. I said I had. Dan said the judge was going to put "my ass in there" and if I was nice to him, he might help me get out.

When he came back, the judge ruled with us. That ruling probably saved years of appellant work and did nothing to undermine the decision to make me the lead counsel.

We were now in a position where we could take the depositions to perpetuate the testimony. We started at the bank at a desk under the staircase. At the depositions, there was a man from the Internal Revenue Service, the attorneys and the court reporters, Conklin and Harold.

At one point, I asked the lawyers to produce the list of this fabulously wealthy man's assets and all the books to support it. In reply, I was given this explanation:

When Mr. Moody's wife died, he became the executor of her estate and cut the property in half. I asked him to produce a list of his assets. They did not have this documented, but the next day they did produce a spiral binder, or composition book of a kind used in grade school, listing the assets. There was no supporting evidence. Mr. Moody, they claimed, had destroyed everything after the split was made.

This is the way Mr. Moody operated: If you had a ranch and banked somewhere other than a Moody bank, he would send his "boys" out to see you. One was a Dallas banker, whose task was to see how many accounts you had, how many head of cattle, how much hay, how much money you had borrowed on the land — everything he could learn. Then, about six months before your note became due, Mr. Moody would ask you to come to his bank and offered to loan you money, telling you how many improvements you could make on your ranch, a new fence or more cattle. The old man would tell you what their interest rates were. The rancher would take the bait and when the note became due, Moody either called it or took your ranch away. No matter how the rancher pleaded with him, W. L. Moody never backed down.

In the depositions, it developed that Mr. Moody rarely missed an angle in his business or social dealings, as these stories will illustrate:

He invited the families of his employees to his ranch to shoot all the quail and game birds they could. When they left, he rewarded them with a brace of fowl and sold the rest at market.

His cooks prepared a huge meal for guests who stayed for dinner. Sitting in the middle of the table, in a prominent position, was a large, porcelain pig. When anyone asked for seconds, he would point the pig at him.

William Lewis Moody, Jr. had three children, Mary Moody, Shearn Moody and William "Bill" Lewis Moody III. One son, Shearn, owned the local Texas League baseball team, the Galveston Buccaneers. Shearn also had two sons, a namesake and Bobby Moody.

The younger Shearn Moody enlisted in the armed forces in San Antonio, lived at the famed Gunter Hotel, and kept two cars parked at the curb, pointed in opposite directions. Which car he picked depended on where he was going. He won favor with his fellow soldiers by taking them to places they had never been.

The other brother, Bobby, was the most conservative. When he had all he ever needed, he bought the cheapest suits and clothes. Shearn was the spender, the playboy. He was also the one who died young.

During the depositions, Fulbright and Crooker were retained by Libbie Moody Thompson, Moody's younger daughter and the wife of a congressman, Colonel Clark Thompson. We did all of the discovery and all of the work, while the Fulbright attorney, Jack Vaughan, sat in on the hearings. On occasion, he was joined by Leon Jaworski. They took no part in them, but listened intently. At one point, we were in the Jean LaFitte Hotel taking depositions, and one of the lawyers sat in a chair and it collapsed. I suggested that he send the bill to Mary Moody Northen.

Finally, I walked into the courtroom one day and someone said a settlement had been reached on behalf of Libbie Thompson. I said, fine, because now they would have to settle with our client, William L. Moody the III, as well.

When we dug our way through all the paper, it turned out Mr. Moody had left about multiple wills, each of them bequeathing his son one dollar. Half a dozen wills would have to be broken, not just one. We finally settled the case in excess of a million dollars, so to go from a buck to over a million was not too shabby — not in those days. (The other boys, Shearn and Bobby, settled later.)

One idea that came out of the settlement, and I do not mind taking credit for it, was a new tax wrinkle. We wanted to spread the payment of our fee over a period of time, but no one knew exactly how to do it. I devised a plan that I thought was foolproof and the

IRS could not contest it. We signed a contract with Bill Moody for a percentage of the recovery. The contract also provided that Moody would have the option to pay us in full, or defer the payment up to ten years.

When the case was settled, we notified Moody and he wrote us that he opted to pay us over ten years, so we received the fee in ten equal installments.

The rift between William L. Moody, Jr., and his namesake, was a predictable one. Bill was very astute, and the most gentlemanly of all the Moodys. He made money in the stock market and saw the flush times coming in Galveston. He purchased a piece of property and built the Jack Tar Courts, which would compete with his father's hotels. Bill was going to borrow the money from his father's bank. One day, his father called Bill into his office.

His first question was, would they be air conditioned? Bill said, yes. An irate Mr. Moody announced flatly that he would not allow it. If Bill went ahead, the old man would be faced with the expense of putting air conditioning units in his own hotels. He asked him where he was borrowing the money, and one can only imagine his agony when the son replied: "From your bank." He was financing his own undoing.

From that moment on, he thundered, Bill could hustle for the money because he would not get another penny from the Moody bank. He went to a rival bank in Galveston, arranged a loan for the remainder, and opened in spite of his father.

In the end, W. L. had to air condition his hotels. Later, he forced his son into bankruptcy, after Bill and a partner had overextended themselves in the oil fields, and by trying to buy the Espersen Building in Houston. After the bankruptcy, he bounced back, but it took Bill Moody III eight to ten years to become a millionaire again.

The old man's final revenge was bequeathing him the dollar in his will.

RIO GRANDE JUSTICE

Long after the west was tamed, the phrase "frontier justice" was still not spoken lightly in Texas. I handled another, unusual estate case in Rio Grande City, in Star County, involving the Guerra family. Of their four sons, one was an attorney and three worked in the family business.

The original Guerra, the patriarch of the clan, had amassed a fortune largely in land, and according to hearsay he acquired much of it by theft and cheating his neighbors. This was confirmed later, when we were ready to settle the case. No money would change hands without a survey of his land, which he resisted. He finally settled without a survey and I believe he got the money out of an unincorporated bank, and because the attorney who represented him was well known in San Antonio.

One of the Guerra boys was kind of rattle-brained and inept, not a hard worker like the other three. He married a lady the family did not approve. They had a child, a boy, and eventually the weak brother died and his widow and son left town.

Notwithstanding the fact that the grandparents lived apart, the elder Guerras encouraged the boy to spend his summers with them. Now Mama Guerra had died. The boy had grown to manhood and, as we pick up the story, he was my client.

The old couple had promised to provide for him in their wills. From the testimony in the depositions I took, it was clear that the grandmother insisted on keeping this commitment, but the old man opposed her. Mrs. Guerra was on her deathbed when the will was signed, and he sent everyone out of the room except the nurse.

When everyone returned to the room, the signature was on the will. Whose signature appeared on the paper was in question: hers, his or the nurse's? The witnesses had witnessed it after the fact. An attorney had been employed by one of the brothers to contest the will and claim the share that would otherwise have gone to the grandson. They had taken the position that the deceased brother, the boy's father, had forfeited his interest by borrowing against his share of the estate.

A local attorney had asked me to handle the case. I asked him why he didn't try it himself. He said he was afraid. The Guerras had a reputation of settling their differences by bringing someone from across the border and liquidating the opposition. I checked out every place I slept and never slept in the same place twice.

In our investigation of the case, the nurse who attended the wife gave us a statement that old man Guerra had signed his wife's name to her will when everyone was out of the room.

Prior to the prelimanary hearing we determined that the Guerras had kidnapped her and taken her to Roma although I had taken the precaution of placing her in the sheriff's custody in the county where she lived.

I told my investigator, Lloyd Barber, an ex-FBI man, trained under J. Edgar Hoover, to find the nurse and make her available for trial. He found her and when she testified, she disavowed and testified contrary to her statement.

The grandmother's will left everything to the brothers. The three living brothers had divided the share of the deceased brother, the father of the grandson I represented.

Now, twenty years later, the grandson had returned to claim his fortune.

Suspecting from the start that the will was a forgery, I hired a man named Appelt, who was considered the foremost handwriting expert in the world. Based in Washington, D.C., he had been a member of the FBI and had set up the school where agents were taught the various ways a document could be forged.

The lawyer on the other side was from San Antonio and had been an FBI agent himself. As the preliminary hearing drew near, he wrote Appelt and said he suspected that Parks was going to bring in some bank teller to claim the will was a fake. He asked if Appelt would prepare a set of questions he could use on cross-examination?

Mr. Appelt received the letter on the eve of his departure for Texas. He wired back that he was going

179

out of town and would be unable to help. He flew down and showed me the letter.

I don't know when the other lawyer recognized who my witness was, but I put Appelt on the stand and held back a little ammunition for re-direct examination. In his cross examination, the opposing lawyer asked if he could see the signs of *arteriosclerosis* in the signature. The answer was no. "Did you see the signs of *senility?*" Appelt then gave one of the greatest answers I have heard a witness give. "No," he said, "but I saw the signs of forgery." A genuine signature cannot be accurately traced and when analyzed it will show irregularities.

I asked if there was anything uncharacteristic about the typewriter used to draft the will. He said yes. I sent my investigator to the office of the Guerra brother who was a lawyer. He obtained a sample from the typewriter and Appelt said that was the typewriter.

We subpeoned and brought the typewriter into trial and a sample from the Guerra typewriter was later identified by Mr. Appelt as the typewriter that the forged will was written on and proved that the forged will was written on that typewriter.

I had filed a motion to force the Guerras to produce their accounting records. As a result, the judge separated this part of the trial and moved it from Rio Grande City to Alice, for the hearing. During the recess, I came back to Houston and shortly received a call from opposing counsel. He mentioned the name of a lawyer he had just hired, who would be known to everyone on the jury, and had never lost a case in that county. With the assurance of a man who had played his trump card, he said, "Fred, you might as well settle. You can't win down here."

I had a problem. And I knew how to solve it. After some deliberation, I called Archie Parr, who had gained a certain notoriety in connection with the 1948 election in Texas, and the votes from Box 13, in Duval County, that sent Lyndon Johnson to the U.S. Senate (by a margin of 87 votes.) The Parrs had built an empire in that part of the state.

I drove out to his ranch and told Archie I wanted to hire him, and all I wanted him to do was to come in and help select the jury, and watch them to see they were not tampered with.

The other lawyer kept pressuring me for a settlement, and I declined, telling him I had hired an attorney to assist me and was quite willing to continue. He asked me his name. I said it was none of his business.

We had a hearing in Alice, and I was reminded again that it pays to keep your eyes open. The attorney for the Guerra family was arguing that the records conclusively showed that the dead brother's portion of the estate had been conveyed to his siblings in settlement of his debts. The attorney had to step over his briefcase and his papers were spread out on the podium. On top of the pile I noticed a letter that said: "I will bring all of the original records in a pickup and have them at the courthouse in case you need them."

I told my investigator to watch the front of the

courthouse, and see what vehicles are parked there. If he spotted a pickup truck, look around and see what might be inside. Back in the courtroom, he whispered, "They have a truck loaded with file boxes."

I had to take a shot in the dark. I said to the judge, "I have reached the conclusion, based on my investigation, that these brothers have kept two sets of books, one for the government and one for themselves. If the court permits, I think you should inquire of their attorneys, as officers of this court, if they actually lied or deceived the court — that the records they produced were the "incorrect ones". The judge meditated for a moment and asked if they had two sets of records. They finally said, "Yes". The judge ordered them to produce the real records, and they did so, after a few minutes that resembled mice scurrying from a broom closet.

Subsequent to the hearing we were able to reach a settlement of the case and the grandson later received his proportionate share of the estate.

DIAMONDS AND BEER DON'T MIX

As I look back over my career, the best times always seem to be when we were young and starting out and knew all the answers, never mind the questions.

When I was still a college student, I worked at the World's Fair in Chicago as a guide. I heard a voice I recognized — I have always been able to recognize voices and faces, although at times I may not be able to attach a name to them. I walked around the partition that separated us and shook hands with Gavin Ulmer, the head of the South Texas Law School. He urged me to return to Houston and finish my education.

In a few months, I came back to Houston and finished my three years of law school. Ulmer asked me to help him try a lawsuit in which he represented B. V. Christy, who was in the stock and bond business. Sensing the changes that would come with prohibition, Christy went to the Southern Select Beer Company (which had won the Grand Prize in Belgium, and thus planned to name their beer "Grand Prize"), and got the rights to sell shares in Southern Select Beer.

A little old lady put her life's savings in Southern Select, and when it collapsed she sued Christy. The reason it collapsed was that Howard Hughes stepped in and hired a French brewmaster. He breached his contract in order to work for Hughes and brew Grand Prize beer at his new plant.

Without a brewmaster, Christy's deal fell through. Christy was an interesting fellow who wore a rather large diamond on his finger and a diamond stickpin on his necktie. I asked him to remove them during the trial, explaining they would not sit well with the jury.

He refused. "I never take them off," he said.

I replied, "Mr. Christy, I don't have too much experience, but with the facts of this case, I think you'd be making a big mistake." This was a little old lady who lost all her money. And every time he moved, the diamond on his finger and on his tie sparkled and caught the eye of the jurors.

It was truly a case of the blind leading the blind. Sure enough, the plaintiff got a judgment against

Christy and he paid it off. Howard Hughes kept the brewmaster and Grand Prize beer.

HOUSTON'S RICH AND "ROYALTY"

The case started off routinely, if not innocently. Lloyd Barber, an ex-FBI agent and the investigator I relied on in the most difficult cases, came to me with a problem: a Houston law firm had hung him out to dry.

He had been hired in the spring of 1969 by the firm of Woody and Rosen to follow Ljuba di Portanova and dig up any scandal that might be helpul to their client, the Baron Enrico di Portanova, in their pending divorce action.

Ljuba (pronounced Loo-ba) was an exotic woman, a Yugoslavian beauty with black hair and flashing dark eyes. She was tall and athletic and in 1956 played on the women's national basketball team. She used the passport she gained as an athlete to defect from Tito's communist domain, landed in Italy and had small parts in movies directed by Dino de Laurentis.

The baron, whose title was accepted by Houston society the way foreign titles always are, was the grandson of the late Hugh Roy Cullen, who at the time of his death in 1957 was one of the richest men in the world. His millions helped build the University of Houston and the medical center. Enrico's mother was Lillie Cranz Cullen, the second child and oldest of the three daughters of the pioneer oilman.

Di Portanova would battle the trustees of the Cullen estate for twenty years to gain what he felt was his share of his grandfather's fortune. The cases that grew out of this saga attracted lawyers the way a wet jelly bean attracts flies. At one probate hearing, the various parties were represented by eighteen attorneys.

Ricky, as he was known to his friends and female admirers, was suing the estate. He also filed suit for divorce from Ljuba, dropped it and counter-sued after she filed her own petition. Di Portanova and his best friend and business partner, Edward Condon, wound up suing each other, and at least one Houston bank was suing the two of them.

But at this point, in 1968, my interest was related only to the problem of my friend, who had run up a sizable tab trailing di Portanova's wife, and whose bills had gone unpaid by the lawyers. This was the story he told:

He had followed Ljuba across the country to Chicago, where he stood in line behind her at the airport ticket counter. He heard her request a flight to Florida, went to a phone, called the office of Clyde Woody and Marian Rosen and asked if he should continue with his surveillance. He was told to continue tailing her. "I got on the same plane," he said, "and followed her until she shacked up with someone in a condo in Miami overlooking a waterway.

"There was no way to get a view into that apartment except from the inlet, so I called Woody and Rosen again and they said, go ahead, no matter the cost, get the goods on her. I hired a guy who owned a boat with a float, put a camera on it and we took some very revealing pictures from the water. I finished the job, came back and turned in my expenses. They complained about the size of the bill and refused to pay me. I showed them the receipts. What was on my credit cards totaled more money than I had in the bank. They still refused to pay."

After listening to this story, I called Ed Condon, who managed di Portanova's business interests in Houston. I told him I had an urgent matter to discuss with him and that it related to the refusal of attorneys employed by the baron to pay debts owed to my client. If he could give us a brief audience, I said, I thought we could clear up the matter quickly. He invited us to drop by.

We went to Condon's office and Woody was there. I told my client to repeat the account of what he had done to incur his expenses. He started talking and Woody kept interrupting. I told Clyde to let my client have his say, and he continued to make negative remarks. Finally, Condon just turned around, pulled out his desk drawer and wrote a check for the full amount.

I didn't bill my friend for helping him. I thought that was all there was to the incident, but it was not.

Two or three months later, who should call but Condon. He wanted to retain me to represent him in a breach of contract suit against di Portanova. Condon was getting ready to leave for Europe and gave me the details of the dispute.

Condon was a colorful figure in his own right, a handsome character who loved the sweet life. He was once married to Payne Whitney, the socially prominent daughter of Joan Whitney Payson, the original owner of the New York Mets. Ed was in charge of

Trans World Airlines in Italy, when he met Enrico, who was a jewel trader and owned a small shop in Rome.

Knowing of his friend's social and financial connections in the United States, di Portanova sought his advice in 1961 regarding the skimpy financial statements provided him by one of the family trusts. He had been receiving $5,000 a month from the estate since Hugh Roy Cullen's death, but no accounting of the assets. It was at Condon's urging that Enrico and Ljuba moved to Houston to pursue his claim. They persuaded Condon, who by then had fallen on leaner times and was running a Sicilian crate factory, to join them.

In Houston, di Portanova's status took a distinct upward turn. Even without litigation, the Cullen estate paid him a lump sum of more than $800,000 in 1965. A year later, his mother died in New York, where she had lived an eccentric life, dressing like a bag lady and ballooning in weight to nearly four hundred pounds. She left an inheritance of $4.8 million to Enrico and his mentally troubled brother, Ugo.

A few months before her death, Enrico had his mother declared mentally competent so she could change her will to designate her sons as her heirs, rather than her wealth reverting to the Cullens. At the same time, Enrico and his father, Paolo, had Ugo declared non compos mentos, so they could become the guardians of his care and his share of the estate.

In Houston, di Portanova opened an office, managed by Condon, for the purpose of exploring oil and other investments. In fact, they were wheeling and dealing and riding a rising stock market. Enrico talked Texas Commerce bank into loaning him over a million dollars from Ugo's trust, and he and Condon set up a company in Europe called "Saxet" — Texas spelled backwards.

In 1967, shortly before Thanksgiving, Condon left a party and speeding along Sunset Boulevard lost control of his Maserati. He crashed into a tree, was trapped in the wreckage and had to have a leg amputated. After his recovery, the partnership continued and for a time thrived.

In 1969 and 1970, Condon transferred over two million dollars to a private investment bank in Switzerland. The break in their relationship came after Condon told Enrico they had lost $400,000 in one of their deals. A furious di Portanova called his bank in Houston and had Edward's authority removed. In effect, he fired him.

This was where I came in.

It is no longer clear to me when, or if, di Portanova had changed attorneys or simply added the controversial Roy Cohn to his legal team. When he hired Woody and Rosen, the firm was relatively small, and hungry, and best known for having worked with Percy Foreman in the trial of Candace Mossler for the murder of her husband. Candace was acquitted, along with her nephew, Melvin Lane Powers. Their practice was primarily criminal law and domestic relations.

The Houston probate courts decided in favor of the Cullens, not surprisingly, but Enrico's monthly check went from $5,000 to $60,000. His divorce from

Ljuba became final sometime in 1971. He took a new wife, the lovely Sandra Hovas, a Houston girl whose family owned a chain of furniture stores. He had homes in Acapulco, Palm Springs, Rome and Houston.

Legal skirmishing that began in 1961 now continued through the 1970's. Cohn, who first gained public notice as the chief counsel for a committee headed by the late Senator Joe McCarthy, was at the center of the Army-McCarthy hearings, a landmark event in television history.

When we began, the depositions were to be taken at the di Portanova home on River Oaks Boulevard, not far from my own home. (At one time, I lived within a few blocks of people who were involved in some of the most notorious legal cases of the last quarter century: di Portanova, Candace Mossler and Dr. John Hill, who had been accused of causing the death of his wife, Joan Robinson Hill, and was murdered in his own doorway.)

I had brought one of my associates, Bob Hudson, with me to take the depositions. But I made it clear I wanted personally to talk with Roy Cohn. We walked into a scene that looked like a Roman holiday: we were led to the guest house by the pool, where tables of food and wine had been set out for us. In his usual fashion, di Portanova had white wine over ice cubes.

When the depositions started, I looked Roy Cohn in the eye and offered him a prediction: he was not going to do anything in this matter except make a fee for himself. One way or another, Condon had made Enrico a great deal of money. Di Portanova had a speedboat, two Maseratis, a Lamborghini, a Rolls and a King Air Beechcraft. Condon was working on a helicopter deal for him in London. Once, they had rented a yacht, filled it with young girls and spent a week to ten days on the Mediterranean.

Enrico had often boasted of those times, but when I asked about that party on the yacht, in his deposition, he had no recollection of the trip. He had a very convenient memory. His father, Paolo, had his own yacht, two or three cars, and some apartments that he put in his girlfriend's name, to his later regret. Paolo was a shorter version of his son, a suave man with a pencil thin mustache. He was working in Hollywood, a would-be actor, when Lillie Cranz Cullen met him during a visit with her parents to Los Angeles in 1932, and was swept off her feet. He claimed to be a baron and traced the title back to 1740, but the standard reference works on European nobility do not support his story.

We finished the business at hand and Ed Condon left for Mirabella, Spain, where he had a villa. He had taken a temporary job on the Seychelle islands off the African coast.

In due course, Cohn wanted to depose Condon, so I arranged to have him questioned in Mirabella, in my hotel room. I contacted Ben Conklin, a court reporter I knew to be traveling in the Holy Land, and made arrangements for him to meet us in Spain to record Condon's deposition.

All the parties arrived and I spent two or three days with my client prepping him for the procedure. Before we started, I said that I would reserve the right to object to all improper questions and to use in cross-examination any that would be revealing or material at the time of the trial. I then walked out and let Roy Cohn take his deposition, as a show of confidence in Ed Condon.

Eventually, Cohn wanted to take additional depositions from Mr. Condon and indicated that he might discuss a settlement. I went to Monte Carlo, where di Portanova kept an apartment on the second floor overlooking the Hotel de Paris casino. His Rolls Royce was parked outside. The partying would start at about 8:30 P.M. and go on until dawn.

We were there for several days. Certain stations or tables had names on them and Enrico would pass through about 6:30 P.M. each day, buying drinks as he made his rounds. Then he would get in his car and drive off. He was entitled to be present when Condon gave his deposition, and though fitting them into Enrico's busy schedule wasn't easy we got them done.

In happier times, the two of them used to frequent Maxim's restaurant when they officed downtown. I walked in one day while they were at the bar, and Ricky sent over a bottle of wine. Camille Berman, who owned Maxim's, told me later that after I thanked Ricky, he told Camille he might as well buy the wine because in the end he would have to pay for the lawsuit.

After we finished the depositions, I put everyone on an airplane, said our goodbyes and I flew to a golf club at the point off Spain near the Rock of Gibraltar. This is one of the outstanding resorts for the multi-rich in the world. From the air, as you fly in, the greens are a lush shade of emerald, and the traps are as white as milk. I am not certain what they are made of, but it may be crushed marble ground as fine as sand.

The first time I played the course, Eddie Condon with one telephone call made all the arrangements. I stayed at the home of one of the wealthiest men there, well attended by the couple who lived there all year as caretakers. Over the years, I played the course several times. On the other side of the road they've added a mini-course. The pro was Henry Cotton, who had left Portugal. They accommodated a lot of tourists with golf, tennis courts, great dining, the whole works.

We never did settle the case. Eventually, Condon signed an affidavit relieving di Portanova of any obligations to him, and stating he had been previously paid. I can't prove it, but I think I know what happened. I believe Condon and di Portanova decided to settle "under the table", so to speak, and I received no fee. I can't speak for Cohn.

In my judgment, Roy Cohn was a good, tough lawyer who would do whatever was necessary to win a case. The last time I saw him, at one of the Republican dinners for President Bush, he came over to my table, which had four vacant seats, and asked if he and a certain senator could sit with us. At the time, Cohn was in the late stages and dying of AIDS.

I had two other contacts with Cohn in Houston, once by chance at the Remington Hotel, when he brought one or two of his boyfriends with him. The other time was in 1981, in court, when Cohn was challenging the transfer of assets from the Cullen trust to

Quintana Petroleum Company, one of the family businesses. Cohn was assisted by former state senator A. R. (Babe) Schwartz, of Galveston, as his local co-counsel. He was opposed by Joe Jamail, who painted the case as a conflict between the jet setting di Portanovas and the hard-working, homebody Cullens.

Ricky di Portanova never did get an accounting of the estate.

BEHOLD A PALE HORSE

In his book, *Blood and Money,* Tommy Thompson described Ash Robinson as a paradox, and he was surely right about that. "He was, on surface viewing, the stereotypic model of the Texas oil creature," wrote Thompson. ". . . He could read a little Greek and Latin and might hold his own in the company of scholars.

"He was a fine-looking, Southern colonel kind of man . . . Only his eyes betrayed him. They were not the eyes of a man content with his lot."

In the spring of 1969, Ash Robinson had good reason for his discontent. His daughter, Joan Robinson Hill, had died under suspicious circumstances. Her husband, Dr. John Hill, had been indicted in the case on the unusual grounds of murder by neglect.

Dr. Hill was later murdered in his own doorway in the same River Oaks neighborhood where I lived. A block or two away stood the home of Candace Mossler, acquitted (with her nephew) in the murder of her wealthy husband. Although the Mossler killing took place in Florida, these celebrated cases, along with a traditional number of Saturday night cuttings and shootings, at one point gave Houston a reputation as the murder capital of America.

I had represented Ash Robinson over the years in many oil deals. He was by nature what Texans call an ornery man, but he was a splendid client. Within a week of a case being completed, win or lose, Ash would come to the office and ask what he owed. He never questioned the amount, and would write me a check on the spot "for legal services rendered, paid in full to date."

I would become involved in the periphery of the trials that followed the deaths of Joan and Dr. Hill, but the saga touched me in a more personal way. When she was a child, I used to boost Joan onto her horse at the Joe D. Hughes stables, where she was taking riding lessons. She went on to become a champion on the national horse show circuit, and a favorite of the crowds on a horse named Beloved Belinda. They were a gorgeous sight, Joan all sunny and blonde on the elegant, dappled gray mare.

As she grew into womanhood, Joan sought my advice from time to time. During what I later learned was a troubled period in her marriage, she asked if I could dissolve a partnership between her husband and another physician. I had drawn the original partnership papers. Hill had met with Donn Fullenweider, one of the fine young lawyers who worked for me, but neither doctor would budge.

The other partner had accused Hill of using some

of his pictures and claimed the work as his own, while giving lectures on plastic surgery.

I asked their bookkeeper to bring her records to my office when Hill was out of the city. I looked over the files and determined that Hill was, in fact, lying about whose patients were shown in the photos. I then called the attorney representing the other doctor, told him to draw up the dissolution agreement, and I signed as Dr. Hill's attorney. I then wrote John Hill and instructed him to sign the agreement. He did and the partnership was ended.

It came as no surprise when Joan called and said her husband had walked out on her. She wanted to protect her son, Robert, known as Boot, in the event of a divorce. At the time, the Hills owned two Cadillacs. Joan drove one and Dr. Hill the other. When they had separated, he conveniently took Joan's car keys with him.

In preparing to proceed with the necessary legal action, I needed some information from Dr. Hill's office. I asked Joan to go by the office and get the records the next time he left town. She reported that he had taken the records and locked them in the trunk of his Cadillac.

It was then that I discovered she had no keys. I told her that was not a problem. All she needed to do was drop by the Bland Cadillac dealership and tell them she had lost the keys to John's car. I told her to remove the papers and bring them to me, which she did.

The information was interesting, but there was no divorce. Joan was still the wife of Dr. John Hill when she died of a massive infection — or something similar — within three days after she first felt ill. Ash Robinson, and some of Joan's friends, and one or two prosecutors in the District Attorney's office, believed that she might have been poisoned.

She and her husband had reconciled a few months earlier. But all around them, the signs were ugly and nasty. Dr. Hill was living off and on with a woman named Ann Kurth, who would become his second wife. His practice had dwindled to practically nothing. In her eagerness to please him, and keep him, Joan was a bundle of raw nerves.

At one time, she had asked me to review the trust fund that had been set up for her son, Boot. She said she was going to accompany Dr. Hill on a visit to Mexico, and she was afraid he might try to kill her when they got down there. This was chilling talk, but Joan wasn't the paranoid type. I tried to discourage her, telling her it could be difficult getting her body out of Mexico if she did happen to die there.

John Hill had done some plastic surgery for the daughter of one of the richest families in Mexico. As it turned out, they had a pleasant time and Joan returned from the trip safe and sound.

I met with Joan about a week before her death to talk in a general way about her situation. We made an appointment to meet again, informally, on a Saturday. She did not appear. I called the house and was advised by the maid that she was ill and too sick to come to the telephone. On Dr. Hill's orders, she was not to have visitors or even to talk on the phone. The next thing I knew, she had been rushed to Sharpstown Hospital, where she died in the early hours Tuesday.

Ash Robinson had hardly slept for two days after receiving the news of his daughter's death. On the morning of his daughter's funeral, Ash Robinson insisted that I accompany him to the Harris County Courthouse. We met with an assistant district attorney, I. D. McMaster, later a judge, and for nearly an hour Ash spilled out his suspicions: her husband, not normally an attentive man, had served her French pastries a few hours before she was taken ill. He might have injected something into her food, if not directly into her system.

When it became clear that her condition was worsening at an alarming rate, he had her admitted to a small hospital with no intensive care unit. She was treated by two doctors who were unknown to her. Before an autopsy could be performed, her body was rushed to a funeral home and embalmed.

There was no hard evidence here of any wrongdoing, but Ash made McMaster curious enough that he telephoned Dr. Joseph Jachimcyzk, the county coroner, and asked him to go to the funeral home and look at the body. The services were to start in two and a half hours. If need be, the coroner was authorized to stop the funeral.

The vital fluids had been lost during the embalming, but enough organs and tissue samples remained so that Dr. Joe could conduct a belated autopsy. He found no traces of any metals, meaning no poisons, such as arsenic. The closest he could come to establishing a cause of death was "viral hepatitis." None of the doctors Ash Robinson consulted agreed with this conclusion.

Within hours, if not minutes, it was all over town that Ash had been to the district attorney's office, in the company of Fred Parks. In *Blood and Money,* I was referred to as a "silk-stocking lawyer." By then I had my share of well-to-do clients, that's true, but I don't think all the oil field workers and widows I represented over the years would have understood the term.

The funeral turned out to be one of Houston's major social events. An overflow crowd used up all the temporary folding chairs and spilled out into the driveway, listening to the broadcast of the service over loudspeakers. Vans delivered more than two hundred floral arrangements.

After the service, Ash and his wife, Rhea, climbed into the first black limousine in the procession. When Dr. John Hill approached the car, Ash locked the doors, told him he could not ride with them and to find another way — which he did.

There was no shortage of rumors, theories, plots and grand jury hearings in the months to come. To further the investigation, Ash sent me to New York to retain that city's famed chief medical examiner, Dr. Milton Helpern, to exhume the body and perform yet another autopsy. We met at the Waldorf Astoria Hotel, agreed on a fee and scheduled his trip to Houston.

The body was exhumed. The focus of his examination was to find any overlooked needle marks in unlikely places, such as under a fingernail. None were found. Neither was the brain of Joan Robinson Hill. It later turned up in a plastic container in the car trunk of the Sharpstown pathologist. He had removed it initially to study, he said. Now he was in the process of transferring it and other specimens from one lab to another.

Between the death of Joan Robinson and the trial of John Hill, the doctor married and then divorced Ann Kurth. It was her theatrical testimony that led to a mistrial.

Prior to the trial, Ann Kurth had called and discussed my representing her. I declined because I suspected it was a set-up with Dr. Hill against me. But her story was remarkable. As their brief marriage began to break down, she claimed that he tried to kill her by crashing her side of the car into a concrete bridge near the stable where Joan had kept her horses. She said he also tried to jab her with a needle, but when the glare of headlights indicated a car was approaching he threw the syringe out the window.

At that point, the judge threw the case out of court.

Before Dr. Hill could be tried again, he was gunned down in his doorway by a hired assassin, while his third wife looked on. Ash Robinson's obsession with his daughter's death led some to suspect that his money had paid for the killer's services. Later, the murder gun was found and the assailant was identified, but he in turn was killed — in an unrelated police shootout — before any meaningful evidence could be obtained. Two women were convicted and sentenced to prison for soliciting the gunman, but neither of them implicated Ash Robinson. He and his wife lived their last years in Florida, in declining health, cut off from their only grandson. I represented him in a couple of oil and gas matters, including one rather large, hotly contested claim.

The last time I saw Robert (Boot) Hill was at a court proceeding in which I had to testify. When I got off the stand, I took Boot aside. I told him I had known him since he was born, and I wanted him to know that in my heart there was no question that his grandfather did not have his father killed.

But this story was, for this family, truly the equivalent of a Greek tragedy.

INDONESIA: Striking Oil

In anyone's life, there are many passages. Sometimes, if we are diligent and lucky, good fortune sneaks up on us when we least expect it.

It was around 1968 that Haden J. Upchurch, a fellow member of the Houston Club, consulted me about a matter involving an oil and gas partnership, managed by Roy Huffington. I agreed to represent him.

Both were graduates of the University of Texas, were former employees of the old Humble Oil and Refining Company and friends of long standing. A tall, lanky, rather striking man, Huffington was highly regarded as a geologist, with a talent for business and fund raising. Upchurch had a law license but never practiced. He was a landman, as that term is understood in the oil industry.

They had gone their separate ways when Roy formed Huffington, Incorporated, in 1958, with himself as the only stockholder. He served as chairman of the board, president and treasurer. The other directors were either attorneys or employees.

The company became involved in a number of activities, including shrimping, a processing plant, real estate and oil and gas programs. It was through the latter that Huffington would make his fortune. He would put together oil and gas "prospects," drilling ventures he regarded as worthwhile, and secured funds mainly from those in a position to enjoy the tax benefits. If the wells paid off, the investors took the income until they got back their financing, plus interest, plus a reduced share of future profits.

In general, these programs provided for a certain portion of the money to be allocated to Huffington, Inc., to cover expenses. In the event the property proved productive, the company was permitted to invest and did so. In 1963, Roy Huffington contacted his friend, Haden Upchurch, and asked his opinion regarding a landman he might consider hiring.

Upchurch suggested himself, and became an employee of Huffington, Inc., that year. R. E. Warren was already with the company as chief geologist and, in 1964, Paul T. Scott was hired as their production engineer.

As an incentive to these key employees, Huffington, Upchurch, Warren and Scott, the corporation entered into written agreements giving each employee a percentage of the earned reversionary interests. Under the terms of the agreement, it was renewed in writing for the years 1966, 1967 and 1968. It was not renewed in 1969 and the partnership expired by its own terms at midnight, December 31, 1968.

The key point, however, was the fact that it was in force during the critical year of 1968.

A change in the tax laws appeared to adversely affect the arrangement that Huffington, Inc., was operating under, so Roy began channeling his drilling ventures into a partnership called Huffington Associates. (As it turned out, the tax decision was not to be a threat.)

Retained as consultants for Huffington, Inc., the employees of the new partnership continued very much as they had in the past. Each occupied the same office, performed the same duties and were compensated by partnership draws in the same amount as their previous salaries.

Also, the partnership was established so as to permit each of the parties to share in the earned reversionary interest at the same rate they had previously enjoyed. In round figures, Huffington, as the managing partner, received fifty-seven percent, the others fourteen percent each.

Huffington Associates continued on with varying degrees of success, with revenues of two to three million dollars in some years, and in others a million or less.

One day, Roy returned from a business trip and related to his partners an intriguing encounter. On his flight, he happened to sit next to retired military man, a General Sprough, of Virginia International. They discovered their mutual involvement in oil and gas. It developed that Sprough had contacts in the Indonesian ministry and he suggested that the two of them might take a trip together to Indonesia.

Huffington volunteered that he never had much confidence in these foreign deals, but each of the partners advised him to take the trip with Sprough and see what transpired. In the meantime, they would tend to business on the home front.

Armed with this encouragement, Roy Huffington contacted Sprough and they arranged the first in a series of meetings in Indonesia. Within a short time, he returned to Houston with a very favorable report on his trip.

After one of Huffington's early journeys, Upchurch asked him whether the partnership was included in the Indonesian deal. Huffington replied, "No."

On August 8, 1968, during the existence of the partnership, Huffington obtained a production-sharing contract and the investors supporting the contract were in the following interests: Golden Eagle Ltd. 35%, Union Texas 35%, Austral 10%, Virginia International 10%, and Huffington 10%. In addition, Huffington and Virginia International had an additional 1% overriding royalty interest which was to cut in for a 12.5% working interest when all of the investors got their money back. When the override cut in, all ownership had to be reduced 25%, thus, Huffington's 10% became 7.5% and then was increased to 20% by a 12.5% override which became a working interest

Throughout the controversy that was soon to unfold, Upchurch maintained he was entitled to his partnership share in the Indonesian venture. During those negotiations, he and Scott were trying to conduct business as usual in Houston; Warren having resigned from the partnership during these negotiations.

Upchurch, however, confronted his old friend. Huffington told him that all of the money that had been spent was his. Haden reminded him that they had a partnership. If Roy would tell him how much his share was he would write a check because he wanted to participate in the Indonesian deal. Huffington ignored him. He terminated the partnership, got the concession and then began the laborious task of finding investors who would enable him to start drilling.

In the sale to Golden Eagle and others, Huffington and Virginia International each retained a one percent overriding interest that would convert to a twelve and a half percent working interest when all of the investors got their money back. This meant that Huffington's original ten percent would be equal to a twenty percent working interest.

In addition, Huffington obtained from the other investors a one percent override as his compensation for putting together the deal. This royalty would not kick in until all of the investors had recovered their money. The override meant, in effect, that the working interest of each of the original investors would be cut back by one-fourth.

This was not an uncomplicated deal, and it serves no purpose to belabor the intricate details. Simply put, the stakes were enormous.

To begin with, Indonesia has fascinated Americans for generations. The Southeast Asian country consists of more than thirteen thousand islands, and many of them have found their way into the realm of legend and folklore.

Jakarta is the capital, and served as the backdrop for the movie, "The Year of Living Dangerously." Bali was celebrated in song, stage and screen, inspiring James Michener's great work, "South Pacific." The eruption of the volcano on Krakatoa, in 1883, killed some thirty-six thousand people and ranks as one of history's great disasters.

When the oil concession was granted, in 1968, Suharto, who had fought against the Dutch for Indonesia's independence, had just become president. He succeeded Sukarno, who had ruled the country for twenty-years as "President for Life," until the anti-communist forces drove him from office.

So it was against this background that the oil explorers came calling. The instincts of Huffington as a geologist were brilliant. The concession with Indonesia covered a total of five million acres. After aerial photos were taken, Huffington drew a sketch of an area about two and a half miles wide and five miles long, and said, "We'll drill here."

They drilled thirty wells and never hit a dryhole.

But success and profits were a long way off when Haden Upchurch decided to fight for what he believed were his rights.

Upon refusal of his last demand, Upchurch directed me to proceed with a lawsuit. In brief: he asserted breach of the partnership contract; a breach by Huffington of the fiduciary relationship of a partner, especially a managing partner; fraud and conspiracy to defraud; breach of trust between Huffington, Inc., and Huffington Associates; and that the production sharing contract was a partnership asset by virtue of its own terms; and that Huffinton, Inc. held legal title to the asset as agent and nominee of Upchurch, et al.

All negotiations at that time were very confidential, and proprietary, and it was almost impossible for me to get any information. I succeeded in obtaining a pipeline into the company and on the 31st day of October, 1969, I filed suit on behalf of Upchurch, in the 161st District Court of Harris County, Texas.

I had never met Roy Huffington before this suit. We had taken depositions, and were trying the case, when I happened to bump into him at the Houston Club. I made a point of telling him, "There is nothing personal in this. I have nothing against you or your family or your company. I just think you got some bad advice. Mr. Upchurch is my client and I'm doing my best to represent him."

He smiled and said, "Well, it looks to me like you're doing a darned good job of it."

Years later, as I became active in Republican politics, I bumped into Roy a few times. He was ambassador to Austria under President Reagan, and we visited with him on a trip to that country. (The wealth he created, largely out of the Indonesia project, made it possible for his son Michael, to spend twenty-five million dollars in a losing race for the U. S. Senate in 1994.)

My motion for a summary judgment was heard by Judge George Cire in April of 1974, which would have awarded us damages on the weight of the evidence. He denied the motion and later invited me into his chambers. Judge Cire had been in my office for five or six years and we knew each other well. He complimented me on my argument. I said, "Judge, if the argument was so good, why did you not find for me and my client?" He just laughed.

But we won the suit. The verdict recognized the rights of Upchurch to his working interest and royalty. Huffington's lawyers appealed and an opinion was handed down by the Court of Appeals almost a year to the day.

Judge Curtis Brown wrote the opinion, and it not only upheld the trial court, but awarded Upchurch the interests abandoned by Warren and Scott. This judgment was a considerable shock to the defense; partly because Brown had been a partner at Baker and Botts, whose firm was representing Huffington.

The lawsuit was working its way to the Texas Supreme Court, and I would be faced with making some interesting moves. I knew that the other side would file a voluminous number of motions, and I would be swimming in paper. I needed an associate appeals attorney and I was afraid to approach anyone in Houston for two reasons. One, much of the information regarding the Indonesia project was still classifed. And two, I had no way of knowing which firms had lawyers who might be connected to the other parties in the Huffington venture.

I went to Fort Worth and made an appointment with Tiny Gooch, one of the great trial attorneys of Texas. I told Tiny that I wanted to hire his firm, Cantey and Hanger, to help me do the briefing on the appeal. I told him I had no monies to advance, but if we won, they would get three times their normal fee. If we lost, they would only get their expenses back.

I assured them I had no intention of losing because I had the law on my side. Gooch said he would have to present my proposal to their steering committee, and I learned later that Mr. Cantey himself swung the vote. "I say we take it," he told his associates. "Fred will have the law and it will just be a matter of organizing the appeal."

I asked them to furnish me with the best legal talent they had for appellate work. They assigned to me Sloan Blair, who has been my friend ever since and, in my opinion, the outstanding appeals lawyer in Texas.

I sent Sloan all the necessary materials for the case and pointed out that I had presented, in my trial brief, an opinion by Chief Justice Cardoza, when he was on the Court of Appeals in New York, in **Meinhard vs. Salmon**. In part, the opinion said:

"Joint adventurers, like co-partners, owe to one another, while the enterprise continues, the duty of the finest loyalty. Many forms of conduct permissible in a workaday world for those acting at arm's length are forbidden to those bound by fiduciary ties. A trustee is held to something stricter than the morals of the market place. Not honesty alone, but the punctillo of an honor the most sensitive, is then the standard of behavior. As to this there has developed a tradition that is unbending and inveterate. Uncompromising rigidity has been the attitude of the courts of equity when petitioned to determine the rule of undivided loyalty by the 'disintegrating erosion' of particular exceptions. Only thus has the level of conduct for fiduciaries been kept at a level higher than that trodden by the crowd. It will not consciously be lowered by any judgment of this court . . ."

Eloquent words, and a message to all who would exercise power.

A few weeks after Sloan was made available to me, I went to his office and told him that I wanted to hire another attorney to help us on the appeal. You could see from his body language — he went rigid all over — what went through his mind. He took it as a signal that I did not think he was good enough to head up the appellate work.

He asked who I was thinking of hiring and I said, "Judge Robert W. Calvert."

Sloan visibly relaxed and said it would be an honor to serve with him. Judge Calvert had just retired from the Supreme Court of Texas and always had been held in the highest esteem.

I told Sloan I wanted to hire the judge on the same basis I had hired his firm, but with one restriction: I did not want him to sign a paper or to appear to be a part of the team. He would primarily arbitrate any differences of opinion between Sloan and me on this appeal. Blair agreed and we went to Austin, where Judge Calvert accepted my offer.

I asked him to write a profile of every member of the state Supreme Court — I wanted to know who were the equity judges and who were not. He wrote a profile of every member of court. Then I knew which ones were law judges as opposed to equity judges.

Calvert was impressed with the Cardoza opinion and said we were on the right track. Sloan wrote the briefs in the Court of Civil Appeals and we argued the case.

As we prepared to argue before the Supreme Court, what I expected happened. Baker and Botts filed an excessively long brief, citing cases in jurisdictions all over the United States. They contended that if a business opportunity is submitted to a corporation and they are not financially able to take care of that proposition, then any of the board of directors can take the deal, on an individual basis, and there is no conflict of interest.

They drew this analogy to the Huffington partnership, in the arguments that were finally heared by the Supreme Court. This was the only time Sloan and I had a difference of opinion, on who would argue our case. Each thought the other should.

None of this was modesty or a lack of nerve. I felt Sloan had an advantage because he had done the almost endless case reading. We met in Austin and made our pitches to Judge Calvert. He said, "Fred, this argument is not going to be a legal one. It is going to be a factual argument and you know the facts better than Sloan. In my opinion, you have to make the argument," which I did.

I had been privy, in an extraordinary way, to the appointment of one of the justices, St. John Garwood.

I was sitting in his law office in Houston one day when the governor called and told him he had been appointed to the court to fill a vacancy.

It was Judge Garwood who, during the arguments, asked how I would answer all of the cases the Baker and Botts attorneys had submitted. I said, "Your Honor, they have presented cases from many jurisdictions, all of which are good law, but they do not cover our case. Our case involves a partnership, which provides that Roy Huffington was the managing partner and owed to his co-partners the highest fiduciary duty recognized by law.

"For instance, he could have taken title to this in the Humble Oil and Refining Company's name and he would have still owned it. But he elected to take it in his own company. As to financing, it is self evident. He financed it for himself. He could have just as easily financed it for the partnership."

Upon leaving the courthouse, we went back to Judge Calvert's office and he took us to lunch. As we entered a building, Dick Miller and Roy Huffington were leaving and saw us with Calvert. When I got back to Houston, Miller called me.

He said, "You SOB, you hired Calvert. You knew Calvert had coffee with the members of the Supreme Court almost every day when he sat on the bench, and even now."

I said, "Dick, are you trying to say that the fee I paid Judge Calvert was sufficient for him to corrupt the Supreme Court? Make up your mind because, if that is what you are saying, I will make it public. The trouble with you is, if you had thought of it first it would have been a great idea."

The Supreme Court handed down a decision in January of 1976. The decision severed our claim to the shares of Warren and Scott on the grounds they were not parties to the suit and remanded it for a new trial, but affirmed the remainder of the judgment.

We retried the case in the district court of Harris County. During the trial Miller never spoke to me, although we were friends of sorts. Before my final argument, he paid me an unusual compliment, acting as if William Jennings Bryan had risen from the dead to oppose him. He implored the jury to rule on the facts and "not to listen to that white-haired man." I believe they did both. We won our case. The judgment also found that Warren had abandoned his interest, but Scott had not. Upchurch, therefore, recovered only his proportionate share out of Warren's interest and nothing out of Scott's.

I would have been entirely satsified with the verdict, except for one ruling. Judge Lewis Dickson, of the 125th District Court, required that Haden Upchurch pay his proportionate share of the cash calls, notwithstanding that the case was on appeal. I implored the judge not to saddle Upchurch with this burden, until the case was settled, but to no avail.

Twice I had been denied a clear victory by judges with whom I had close relations, and I think that says something about the integrity of the law. Judge Cire had overruled my motion for a summary judgment, and now Lewis Dickson had given me, in effect, half a loaf.

Both instances tend to support the ideal that justice is blind. Lewis Dickson had been my friend for many years and we were for a time partners in the transportation business. We had obtained the first frozen food carrier in Texas. We were close enough that we attended the same parties at Christmas, and one year Lewis and I played catch with footballs he and Price Daniel were giving to their kids.

Another time we closed up Percy Foreman's annual Christmas bash. Percy gave me the key to his liquor cabinet and told me to keep the party going as long as we wanted. After the last guest passed out, Lewis and I took four quarts of whiskey from Percy's cabinet and made a night of it.

But in the courtroom, you check your friendships at the door. When the jury came in, Judge Dickinson was reluctant to enter the judgment. We had two or three meetings where the ruling was discussed by both parties. I was arguing to relieve Upchurch of the obligation to pay the working interest calls during appeal.

I said it was intolerable, and pointed out that the judge knew this because he had been in the oil and gas business. I doubted that we could get the financing. But he was adamant, and said, "Do you want this judgment or do you want me to declare a mistrial?"

He entered the judgment, and almost before the ink was dry Baker and Botts wrote us a letter demanding payment and threatening forfeiture if we unable to pay. I called them and said, at least, they could give us the courtesy of waiting for the judgment to become final.

The appeal was denied and the litigation, which had begun in late 1969, was at long last ended in October of 1980.

We made arrangements to finance our obligations during and after the appeal. Later, the company bought his working interest and took an option on his override. Eventually, they dropped the option, which turned out to be a short-sighted move on their part. So Haden received money up front, and still gets income from the override.

Originally, we had a call once a month. Subsequently, the call came once a week. Not a great deal of money was involved while they were just developing the field. As time passed, there was some suspense about getting the money to meet the payments. I understood that there was an office pool at Baker and Botts, with the pot going to the fellow who picked the day I failed to bring the monthly payment. I would actually take a cashier's check to Huffington's office.

But I made the payments, and for over a year I kept making them. There was no certainty as to how long it would take before the venture turned a profit. But I was betting on what I knew: the Japanese had loaned Indonesia half a billion dollars to build a plant. With delays and overruns, the final cost was over a billion. I figured something valuable had to be there.

At one point, I signed a contract to sell my working interest to our lenders — that's how troubling it had become to keep getting the money. We shook hands and I thought it was a done deal. The next day they said they had reconsidered and would only go forward if I included my override. I told them, no, and the deal was off — the best deal I never made.

Later, they tried to hijack my override. It was my custom to pick up a cashier's check at their office, deliver it to Huffington's secretary and get a receipt before the end of the working day. This time, they said they were withholding the payment unless I sold them my override.

I went to the phone, called Huffington's secretary and asked her how late she would be in her office. She said as late as 5:30 P.M. I asked if she would do me the courtesy of staying until six, that I might be delayed.

Then I turned to our creditors, and said they had better reach in their pockets and come up with a payment. If they didn't, Huffington would foreclose on all of us, and they would be hiring me to represent them in court to reestablish their rights. A few minutes later, they handed me a check.

I retained my working interest and my override, and with a portion of the money established trusts for my grandchildren. The first income check I received was substantial, over a million dollars, and they have been coming in ever since. The agreement with the Indonesian government has been extended to the year 2017. They have been processing a billion cubic feet of gas a day, plus the energy to run four plants. The concession turned out to be one of the richest in history.

Chapter 6

BEHIND THE
IRON CURTAIN

AT THE HEIGHT OF the Cold War, when a trip to Russia was not something taken lightly whatever your profession, Mrs. Parks and I traveled to the Soviet Union.

This was in 1960, long before anyone imagined the collapse of Communism, like the slow motion film of a building being demolished, and long before anyone dared call the Soviet Union "an Evil Empire," just say it out loud, as Ronald Reagan did, two decades later.

Our journey was taken in connection with the bi-annual conference of the International Bar Association, held that year in Salzburg, Austria. Prior to the meeting in Salzburg, we went to Russia in order that I, as a trial lawyer, could visit the courts, have conferences with the lawyers and judges, and observe their trials to attain some knowledge of that country's jurisprudence.

The most interesting single point that I learned

about the court procedures of Russia was the fact that there is no oath and no penalty for perjury in connection with court testimony.

Mabel and I flew into Moscow from Amsterdam in the middle of June, 1960, in a two-pod Russian jet aircraft. We were met at the airport by our Intourist guide and interpreter, a slim, blond girl by the name of Rimma. Intourist is responsible for the visitors' activities, and such activities are contained in limits established by higher Soviet authority.

It did not occur to me then that our presence could in any way involve some level of danger. Yet this was a time when a foreigner, a westerner, was the subject of instant suspicion. If you were not a spy, a seeker of forbidden information, you at least had the capacity to corrupt ordinary citizens with your ideas of democracy and your tales of a bountiful land.

I realized some years later that I may have been viewed with concern because of my insistence on raising questions, and my enthusiasm for a good argument. I would flatly reject some of their claims. These were easily taken as the tell-tale signs of a provocateur.

In each of the cities we visited, a small bus, not much larger than a van, and a driver were assigned to us. Each morning, with one or more Intourist guides, our party of five, consisting of three men and two ladies, one of whom was Mrs. Parks, would board the bus and be driven from place to place, in accordance with the day's itinerary. It was customary for each group to have, as I understood it, just one Intourist guide in each city.

Contrary to this custom, Rimma stayed with us and was joined by additional guides wherever we went. By the time we reached Kiev, I was guessing that we had been identified as a potential problem. We were assigned a man by the name of Vladimir and one additional lady Intourist guide.

From Moscow we traveled via the famous Red Arrow train to Leningrad, a city of distinct beauty, with great squares and parks. The people seem better mannered than those in Moscow, and will point out to you the apartments of Pushkin and Dostoevsky. The train was comfortable, but lacking in amenities. There was only a toilet at each end of the car and no food service. We were, however, served a cup of hot tea in the morning before leaving the train.

From Leningrad we flew a two-engine Convair type plane to Odessa, which is Russia's principal port on the Black Sea, as well as a major industrial city. En route we landed at Minsk, the capital of what was once White Russia, on a muddy dirt airstrip. We took off again in the same ruts.

From Odessa we traveled by boat to Yalta and our accommodations were fine. Rimma was forced to share a cabin with a man she had never before seen. This was the custom. On the deck in a driving rain we saw young people crouching all night in a corner by their suitcases with no cover.

Next we flew to Kiev, a city of a million people and the capital of the Ukraine. Kiev had been nearly destroyed by Nazi air raids and later door to door fighting during the war.

From Kiev we flew to Vienna, leaving behind us the Iron Curtain.

Neither Mrs. Parks nor I spoke Russian. We did have the good fortune to have with us for the entire trip a young linguist by the name of Jim Beaver, who was a graduate of the University of California and spoke fluent Russian. He was a great help, in that we could talk with the people through Jim and have newspapers, public address systems and other written material translated. Through Jim, we were also able to keep a rather close check on the translation done by the interpeters from the Intourist bureau.

These were the conclusions I reached after our journey of eighteen days behind the Iron Curtain. Some have been overtaken by time, but I arrived at them honestly and feel they were valid at the time:

1. Russia is a police state with all that the name implies.
2. The Russians are a Godless race of people. (After the breakup of the Soviet Union, the quick reopening of churches and the reawakening of religious fervor showed that the pockets of faith were deeper than we imagined.)
3. The Russians are an amoral race.
4. The Russians are bent on Communist world conquest, with the United States as the Number One target. Not long after our return, I was invited to speak at a Cold War Strategy Seminar, held at the Cullen Auditorium on the University of Houston campus. There I elaborated on these points, and gave examples and observations that led me to these conclusions.

In 1960, the Russians were not allowed to criticize their leaders or government. He (or she) must express their beliefs within the principles of Lenin and Stalin and, at that time, Nikita Khrushchev. (They have new freedoms today, but lifelong habits are hard to break, and the masses do not easily exercise this right.)

During our trip, when I explained to our guides that in the United States one could criticize the president, or anything else we disliked, Russian guides could not comprehend this and would not admit the right of free speech to voice even a justifiable criticism would be good for the people.

The Russians could not then, nor to some extent today, travel from city to city or leave the country without permission. Vladimir, the Intourist guide, was a lawyer and he told me he would like to have attended the International Bar Association meeting in Salzburg. But he just laughed when I asked why he did not.

Mrs. Parks invited Rimma to visit us in America, and her reply was, "Why, I could never get permission for such a trip."

One morning at breakfast I asked if there was anyplace I could buy a newspaper published in English? The answer was, no, but I was advised that I could go to the library and read one. I then asked if a Russian had access to these newspapers written in English, and could go in and get one to read. Rimma immediately said, "Yes." But after a great deal of discussion, it developed that the papers in the library were several months old, and before a Russian could read the paper he or she must use their library card, which identified them and their request. This procedure made it unattractive for them to read our papers. I am sure that sanctions would be used to discourage them from such curiosity.

The libraries were stocked with literature that was censored or controlled. The newspapers, radio stations, television stations and the public address systems that we heard extolled only the virtue of the Communist way of life, and almost universally referred to the United States in a derogatory way, such as "the capitalist running dogs" have done thus and so.

There were no public debates between school children or adults on any economic, political or governmental matters. The Communist party enunciated the policy on these subjects.

The working people who were members of unions, and most of them still are, were told when and where they may take their vacations. For example, Odessa, located on the Black Sea, is one of the largest resort and tourist centers, and it has sixty sanitaria and forty rest homes that are visited by some two hundred thousand Russians annually. A great many of these visitors are working members of the various unions.

The currency was, and is, controlled and dominated by the Russian officials. For example, the domestic rate of exchange in 1960 was four rubles to the dollar. For the tourist, such as we were, the rate was ten rubles to one. So the tourist was given two and one-half times more buying power than the average Russian.

Their wages varied from a minimum of some eighty-five American dollars per month up to, we were told, eight thousand rubles or two thousand dollars for a nuclear scientist.

Rimma, our guide, had recently received a raise, she said, from eight hundred to nine hundred rubles a month — or the equivalent of from two hundred to two hundred twenty-five U.S. dollars. In 1960, this is what the Russians had to pay for certain items:

A very low grade men's suit: sixteen hundred rubles or four hundred American dollars.

A table TV set: two thousand rubles or five hundred dollars.

A two-wheeled motor scooter: six thousand rubles or fifteen hundred dollars.

A pair of rather clunky women's shoes: sixty-five dollars.

A plain white man's shirt: twenty-five dollars.

A small-tank vacuum cleaner: a hundred dollars.

Rimma, who now earned two hundred twenty-five dollars a month, would have to work approximately ten days in order to buy a good pair of women's shoes, and these would not be at all fashionable by our standards.

Most of the churches of Russia had long since seen their property and buildings confiscated by the state, and the buildings converted into museums, theaters or warehouses, referred to as "inactive churches." Active churches were the ones in which services were still held.

The Russian masses did not, or were not permitted, to believe in religion in 1960. They had been educated to think that religion was for backward people only, and within Russia I took that to mean the older persons who had been unable to completely assimilate the Communist doctrine.

There were no religious observances in any of the schools or universities. The only people we saw observing any religious ceremonies on our trip were those over fifty years of age, who would have been small children during the last years of the Czar, Nicholas.

We visited a collective farm about fifty miles outside of Odessa, upon which some sixteen hundred people lived and worked. I inquired as to how many of them attended church. I was told by the comrade co-director that at the last Easter services, which any or all could attend if they desired, only three elderly people went. This information was given us in a flippant manner, disrespectful to religion, and was followed by the observation that the Russian people didn't care about going to church.

The youth of Russia were taught by the communists that religion is evil and that atheism is the correct faith.

I recalled that Lenin said, "Give us a child for eight years and it will be a Bolshevik forever." The Soviet creed, in 1960, was Lenin's creed.

In order to be sure of a continuing population schooled in atheism, the young children were placed in the hands of the state during their early years, and the nurses and teachers trained the young child in the ways of atheism, not God.

Russian children between the ages of eight and fifteen years went to pioneer camps during the summer months. These camps were free and there was no religious influence or teaching permitted. The young people we were thrown into contact with, including our Intourist guides, were atheists. They were quite outspoken to Americans concerning their creed, or beliefs, and they were quick to ridicule one's belief in God whenever the subject of religion was made the basis of any discussion.

During one of these sessions, I was asked if I believed in God and I replied, "Yes." The next question was, "Have you ever seen God?" I replied, "No, but I have seen evidences of God even in Russia." I continued with a statement along the lines of, "Notwithstanding the great advancement the Russian scientists have made, they have never been able to reproduce a flower or a leaf and they never will."

I then asked if I could ask them a question about their beliefs? They said, yes, and I asked them if, when Russians felt death approaching, did they pray to Lenin and Stalin, who were lying in a refrigerated glass mausoleum in Moscow? I further observed to them that I knew their prayers to these two men, who I had seen on this marble slab, would avail them of nothing as they were dead.

We were told that the older persons who tried to take their children to church would have some kind of sanctions invoked against them.

We did attend a church service at a monastery some fifty miles from Moscow, in the little village of Zagorsk. We observed only the older women and men worshipping, and as we stood in the church with the old people on their knees, praying aloud, the two

Intourist guides who were with us laughed and commented on the foolishness of such actions.

We were invited into the chapel of the brother in charge, and while visiting with him we asked if we could leave a contribution for his church. Much to our surprise, he politely said, "no," thanked us and at the same time walked over to a drawer at a built-in desk, opened it and pointed to a box that contained money. Although no word was spoken, we knew we were being invited to make a donation.

It was later explained to us that the buildings of this monastery were probably wired, or bugged, and it was for this reason that the good brother would not verbally agree to accept any contributions.

In Leningrad, a city of almost four million people, there were only eighteen active churches. In the Hermitage Museum and Art Gallery, the Louvre of Russia, I asked our Intourist guide to interpret for us the statements of another guide lecturing a group of teen age children, while she pointed to a hammer and sickle that appeared at the North Pole of a large world map.

Almost as a reflex, my guide said she was telling them the Russians discovered the North Pole. I replied, "Is that so? Tell me the name of the explorer and the year of the discovery."

She attempted to change the subject, but I would permit no evasion. Finally, the guide said that the children were having it explained that the Russians sailed the first ice breaker to the North Pole. This was later changed to, "She was telling them about the first Russian ice breaker that reached the North Pole."

In a Russian newspaper, we saw a photograph of a male American teen ager, standing behind a home-made lemonade stand with a sign printed in awkward fashion, saying: "Lemonade 5 cents a glass. The caption said: "This is an example of how the capitalist dogs of America exploit their youth and force them to work and support their parents."

While passing time in the waiting room of the airport at Kiev, for our plane to Vienna, I stepped upon the luggage scales and weighed myself. Soon thereafter, Rimma, our regular guide, became angry when fifty or more Russians lined up and proceeded to weigh themselves.

In Odessa, we met an American citizen named Keller. He had returned to Odessa, where he lived as a boy, having been born a Russian Jew near that city.

The time was rapidly approaching for him to pay Yarzheit, the annual memorial observance of the death of his father, which, I understood, according to their belief, is done by uttering a prayer in the presence of a congregation of ten or more Jews. Mr. Keller spoke Russian and in this city of over one million people he was unable to find a single active synagogue. He finally paid his respects in a synagogue that had the look of a 1930's American speakeasy, located in a basement.

The Russian constitution separates the state, the school and the churches, and the right of religious worship.

In Lengingrad, I remarked that the border that separated Finland and Russia appeared farther away than it was before Russia captured some Finnish territory. The guide said, "We didn't take any Finnish territory," and when I questioned her about it she replied that, "The Finns were killing Russian border guards and in order to protect them they just pushed the Finns back."

Late one night in Yalta, in the Intourist office, four or five guides and I had a rather heated discussion about a variety of subjects, such as Hungary, Berlin and the Voice of America broadcasts. I had been needling them rather hard when one guide shouted, in an angry tone, "If the United States continues their policies, the Russians would be forced to wipe your cities off the face of the earth with thermo-nuclear bombs."

My reply was to the effect that we would retaliate against any overt act, and if they decided to send airplanes to our country carrying bombs, they should be sure to tell the pilots if they flew out of Moscow to select an alternate base before they left. Moscow and the Kremlin would be gone when they returned. Needless to say, this broke up the session.

I was not, I should add, trying to bait or atagonize our hosts. I was genuinely curious about their philosophy and their way of life, and equally eager to answer their questions about ours. At one point, I was asked why America had sent Francis Gary Powers, the U-2 pilot who was shot down over Russia, to spy on their country.

I reminded them of Pearl Harbor and explained that we did not intend ever to be caught napping a second time. Their reply was: "We don't have any spies and never have had, anywhere in the world." To them Julius and Ethel Rosenberg, who were executed for providing the Russians with documents related to the atomic bomb, were symbols of capitalistic propaganda.

Another point of contention was their insistence that the United States did nothing to open a second front, would not help the Russians during the war, and that the Russians without our help withstood a nine-hundred day seige of Leningrad and, unaided, finally defeated Hitler. Their troops, according to the Soviet version, were already in Berlin when the American troops marched in almost unopposed. And since that time, the United States had been attempting to dictate to Russia, as well as the rest of the planet, how to run and govern all the nations of the world.

It may be relatively easy, from the vantage point of the mid-1990's, to attribute much of the distrust of the '60s to political paranoia. But certainly a good deal of it was not unfounded. As we traveled in and out of various airports, I could not help but notice the type of transmitters that are used for jamming radar and radio signals.

When asked if the towers were, in fact, used for this purpose, the answer was invariably, "No, they are broadcasting transmitters." After considerable discussion, and argument, our guides would reluctantly concede that they were jamming stations, but were no longer in use.

After making several requests, I was fortunate to be able to see and photograph the U-2 plane that was on exhibit in Gorky Park in Moscow. The plane had been dismantled and the parts showed very little evidence of a crash. For example, the wings appeared to be rather intact, although full of bullet holes. The camera lens appeared to be unbroken.

At the time we were there, the Public Enemy Number One to the Russians was President Eisenhower, and running him a close second was Vice-President Nixon.

Hitler, or perhaps his propaganda maestro, Josef Goebbels, once said there is nothing, no matter how untrue, that if repeated often enough people will believe it. The Russian communist never tells a lie because what they say is in the interest of Communism and therefore, by his standards, true.

As a general impression, I found the people in Moscow a sad group whose lives were dreary. They were not obsessed with money the way Americans are, not because they were indifferent to material things, but because there was no Russian middle class and no mobility. There were the poor, who stayed that way, and the powerful, whose positions were subject to sudden changes.

There were few cars on the streets of any of the cities, except those used by the higher level of Soviet officials, seen entering and leaving the Kremlin. The average Russian traveled mainly by foot. While trucks were common on the highways, in the city there were some buses, a few taxis and the subway, perhaps their crowning civilian achievement. The subway, or Metropole as it is called in Moscow, was the most beautiful I had ever seen, perhaps the only one in the world that is truly an artistic attraction. There are chandeliers, statuary and mosaics in each of the sixty-five to seventy stations that were first opened in 1935. In 1960, there were four complete lines, three of them crossing the city diametrically and one circling the city. It was maintained principally by women.

The children were friendly, in some ways fearless, especially the young boys between the ages of six and twelve. They were eager to have American chewing gum, Lincoln pennies and ballpoint pens, and would gladly trade you pictures of Stalin or Lenin for these items. I believe that the maturing of the '60s generation was a major factor in the emergence of Glasnost, and then the cataclysmic rejection of Communism. Still, it must be noted, which forces will prevail in today's Russia is an ongoing story.

In Leningrad, Odessa and Kiev the people appeared somewhat happier and moved and spoke with more openness. In Yalta, in particular, there was evidence of laughter and fun on the beaches and around the public refreshment stands.

In reflecting on those times, and in an academic spirit, a word about Russian women is necessary. We observed no evidence that brassieres or foundation garments of any kind or character were worn by them. Most of the Russian women, due to the heavy nature of their food, were unattractive in appearance. They wore drab colored handkerchiefs of squares of cloth on their heads. Their shoes were low heeled, sandal types of poor quality. They wore socks instead of hosiery and Mrs. Parks told me she did not see one woman with a pair of gloves during our entire stay.

Little or no makeup was used and the few beauty salons that we saw, although constantly busy, did not seem to turn out any stylish hairdos. Style was simply not a part of their society. A great deal of the heavy manual labor in Russia was done by women wearing black aprons as they performed their jobs of sweeping the streets, or cleaning and maintaining the public parks.

The men wore suits with wide pants legs, which gave them the same appearance of width from shoulder to shoes. The suits were of a rough quality and very few men wore ties. When you saw one, he looked strangely out of place. Most of the men wore caps instead of hats.

We saw a great many soldiers with a variety of uniforms, but none were very neat. They all had that sack look, as if their clothes had never been pressed, or they had been worn 24-hours a day and slept in.

There was one area where the Russians held a distinct edge over Americans: schools. The entire population, I thought, was encouraged and aided in obtaining an education. Our Intourist guides told us that after the war the people who could read and write went from home to home, and family to family, and taught the older people who had been unschooled. Based upon my observation, and little tests that I personally conducted, I never found an illiterate Russian, even in 1960.

We visited the University of Moscow built on the Lenin Hills overlooking the Moscow River, which was opened in 1953. We were advised that there were presently about eighteen thousand students and a teaching staff of between a thousand and twelve hundred. Part of the classes are still being held in the old location in downtown Moscow. We were not able to make any determination about the university's academic rating, but those students who show a desire to learn are afforded an opportunity to go to school and are paid by the government.

I had no complaints about the air service. The plane that flew us into Moscow was a fine craft, a twin-engine jet that flew at a speed the airline claimed was eight hundred kilometers an hour. The flying time between Amsterdam and Moscow was about three hours. The plane had excellent lounge facilities, adequate space, the stewardesses were polite and efficient, the food plain but good. We landed in Moscow on the longest runway I have ever seen. It must have been some three miles in length, designed I suspected for possible future use by supersonic military bombers.

We found the entertainment in Russia, limited though it was, to be generally good and attended at all times by capacity crowds. We thoroughly enjoyed the two most famous Russian attractions, the circus and the Bolshoi ballet, performing "Swan Lake."

We saw the opera "La Traviota" at the palatial Solshori Theater. The seats were covered in deep red velvet and trimmed with embossed gold. A huge box that was built for the Czars in 1856 bore the emblem of the hammer and sickle. The curtain was made of red and gold silk and had thirteen panels, and on each panel a design in this order: First a lyre, then the initials CCCP, which to us is the USSR, a hammer and sickle and last a red star.

In strong contrast to the elegance of the theater and its settings, the costumes and furnishings, the guests who attended were lacking completely in the kind of gaiety shown by the free peoples of the world at their entertainments. These people wore poor clothing and, due to the lack of ventilation, the odors were rather offensive. During intermission, the people flocked to the refreshment areas where they bought salami and cheese sandwiches and drank vodka, beer and champagne. They returned to their seats eating oranges and apples, dropping the cores and peelings on the floor.

Nothing I saw or heard would have been of benefit to the American military, not that I believe that this was of any real concern to our hosts. But I find it compelling in the light of recent historic events to look back on that trip, and our impressions of the Soviet Union even as the torch was being passed in America. In November, of 1960, two weeks after my speech at the University of Houston, John F. Kennedy was elected to the presidency, defeating Richard Nixon in the closest race in modern times.

Of all our travels across the globe, others may have offered more glamour or more luxury, but none was more meaningful than our eighteen days behind the Iron Curtain.

Chapter 7

AEROBUS by Parks

IN THE MID-1980's, I began winding down my active practice of law, yet I felt fine and eager as ever to seek interesting and challenging opportunities. Making Frank Bernard's acquaintance supplied a decade-long experience at meeting both of these criteria.

Bernard was a highly successful entrepeneur from Vancouver, British Columbia, and a former Canadian ambassador. He had sold three or four hotels in California, owned a residence in the desert near Palm Springs and from all appearances possessed considerable cash.

He also possessed the franchise to market Aerobus systems in North and South America. Aerobus is a short way of referring to a unique Swiss-developed transit technology capable of moving people, and cargo containers, by elevated, suspended, prestressed cable stretched between pylons. Bernard had ridden an Aerobus system which was installed in St. Anne's,

Quebec, Canada, years ago and became instantly impressed with its marketing potential.

The technology was developed and patented in Europe in the early 1970's by Gerhard Mueller, who manufactured ski-lifts in Switzerland. Vevey Engineering, in Vevey, Switzerland (where Charlie Chaplin and his family lived) had acquired the deceased Mueller's rights to Aerobus. They had funded a series of feasibility studies on possible Aerobus projects at various locations around the globe.

Bernard's enthusiasm for Aerobus was contagious. So much, in fact, that I asked for — and he gave me — the state of Texas and surrounding areas as my "territory" for marketing the Aerobus systems.

It so happened that Vevey had made one of its expensive, free feasibility studies for The Woodlands, the highly successful "model cities" developed by oilman George Mitchell, north of Houston. Vevey had sent a representative from Switzerland to do the study, but in the end The Woodlands management did not pursue its initial interest.

In the meantime, a banker in San Pedro, California, Steve Podesta, came on the scene. His interest was in moving containers delivered by ships to the Long Beach port to railroad sidings to be transported to destinations across the country. The potential for moving cargo held no appeal for Bernard, even though Vevey had seriously studied the possibilities. Thus, I hired a person to develop what could be done.

The Long Beach Port officials were willing to consider financing a much needed demonstration test facility ("DTF"). This was a convenient time to show that moving containers by Aerobus, rather than the conventional truck method, was not only feasible, but desirable. But Bernard had the last word, and my vision for a test site in Long Beach went untapped.

Still another opportunity for Aerobus resulted from my attending Canada's World Fair in Vancouver. While there, I met with Bernard and Podesta, both of whom had been working on a prospect of installing a system in a Canadian ski area. I was most encouraged by this pending development. My suggestion to Frank Bernard, as well as to Vevey's man in charge, André Pugin, was that the steps be initiated to take Aerobus "public" through a stock offering.

This move made sense to me not only as a means of raising important startup capital, but as a way to heighten public awareness of this technology.

My attorney in Fort Worth, Sloan Blair, began preparing the necessary paperwork and Bernard came to Texas for the purpose, or so I believed at the time, of expediting the legal effort. As things turned out, however, Frank had talked the Vevey representatives out of the move to go public. Thus, we were right back where we started.

Vevey was not standing still. Interests in Kuala Lampur had summoned Vevey to conduct a study for an Aerobus system for that major southeast Asian metropolis. Vevey personnel completed extensive drawings for the expected installation — everything was in order to proceed and, in fact, construction had actually begun. At the last moment, financing failed though a passenger station had been built. Thus, this Aerobus launch was aborted for reasons having nothing to do with its capability of serving a major city.

I had hired a former Vevey employee to develop possible sales of the systems. He had been in contact with prospects in Athens as well as Israel. But Vevey's commitment to Aerobus, which was just a small corner of that company's business, had begun to wane. For internal reasons, the Swiss manufacturer decided to sell their Aerobus division.

A year passed without a buyer. So, in June of 1987, I made a trip to Switzerland and before returning home André Pugin and I had reached an agreement on my purchase of all rights, including patents, of Aerobus.

Whether one should take on a task of such dimensions, in his seventies, having fulfilled one career and one lifetime, is a subject for philosophers. You are like a man trying to start, at the same time, an airline and a new professional football league. You are fine tuning the equipment, seeking cities, teams, passengers, converts, the perfect playing field.

You prepare yourself for round after round of rejection. You break out of a corner, see an opening; something or someone cuts you off. Ten years will pass. You spend a fortune in dollars, more in time and energy.

It becomes not an investment, but a quest. You can't give up because you believe in it.

So, there was plenty to do once I closed the agreement to acquire Aerobus. One of my first steps was to contact a former Federal Transit Administration engineer, Wolfgang Bamberg. Bamberg was the principal author of a report made by the UMTA (Urban Mass Transit Administration) on an Aerobus system which had operated in Mannheim, Germany, in the early 1970's.

There was a six-month horticulture exposition held in the West German city. The grounds covered considerable space, including lakes. An Aerobus system was installed which carried two and a half million passengers, without incident, for the half year the exposition lasted.

The United States government showed its interest in the relatively new technology by assigning Bamberg the job of analyzing the performance of Aerobus at the Mannheim event.

The report gave Aerobus a thumbs-up verdict and said that the technology represented a viable alternative to conventional mass transit. It was pointed out that the Aerobus guideway (elevated cables and track on curves) could span thousands of feet, with suspension pylons spaced long distances apart.

The U. S. government report helped confirm my own judgment about Aerobus. I was convinced that no transportation system worked as efficiently as Aerobus in highly congestive areas. Furthermore, cost wise, Aerobus is far more competitive than other modes of public transportation. And Aerobus, because of its design, has the capability of spanning rivers or highways or other obstructions, surpassing other technologies in certain applications.

When I became acquainted with Bamberg, around

1987, he was still living in the Washington, D.C. area and was a member of a highly recognized engineering and consulting firm specializing in the public transit industry.

He and I discussed his moving to Houston and establishing an AEROBUS of Texas, Inc., with the objective of marketing the systems. Bamberg actually did some house looking in Houston, but we mutually agreed that perhaps such a step was premature. Nevertheless, in the earliest days of my ownership of Aerobus, Bamberg was my closest adviser and early architect of what was needed to start a successful Aerobus operation in the United States.

He cautioned me to be slow and deliberate in getting underway and I followed his advice carefully. Events pushed me, however, to begin making some significant commitments.

The most important situation was brewing in 1987-88, and remains alive today. One of the places for which Vevey had done one of its feasibility studies was Chongqing, China.

Chongqing (Chiang Kai Shek's capital city in World War II) is a metropolitan area of several million people about three thousand miles deep in the interior of the world's largest Communist nation. Its central city district is divided by both the Yangtze and Jailing Rivers. Like other major Chinese cities, Chongqing is taking the necessary steps to correct its infrastructure deficiencies. Public transportation is high on the city's list of needs.

Its problems are complicated by the river crossings to travel north and south. The city is developing subway and monorail systems, but to cross the rivers some other solution (other than the countless number of bridges) was needed. That is where Aerobus provides the solution. Because the pylons which support the cable along which Aerobus vehicles move electrically can be spaced long distances apart, the Chongqing transportation people became "sold" on an Aerobus installation.

Among the papers, drawings and other materials I obtained upon purchasing Aerobus from Vevey was that firm's preliminary feasibility study for the Chongqing project. That study concluded that Aerobus was suited for the very special circumstances of crossing the two rivers.

Upon learning that Vevey had sold the rights to me, Chongqing officials contacted my office. After several months of correspondence and planning, a delegation of four Chinese engineers from Beijing confirmed they would arrive in Houston for a week in July, 1988.

The engineers were the president and three others from the Central Engineering and Research Institute for Non-Ferrous Metallurgical Industries — referred to as ENFI for short. ENFI had been hired by Chongqing as a consultant to advise the city on the use of Aerobus as one of the legs for a future modern transportation system.

The president, a fine looking, mild-mannered man with considerable dignity, near sixty, was named Yu Mingshun. With him, in their late thirties or early forties, were two engineers, Li Song and Li Xing. The fourth man, who had the title of chief engineer, was a much older person who hardly opened his mouth during the entire time the small group was with us. We speculated that he probably was a Communist party representative, who was along to enjoy a trip to the United States and to be sure that the others were loyal to their mission. As far as we could tell, they were.

What a week! Each day we met around a circular table in the tenth floor library of the Houston Club. We had engaged a consulting firm through Texas Commerce Bank to assist us in negotiating with our Chinese visitors. The firm was a joint venture of the Chemical Bank and a very wealthy Hong Kong investor. The firm sent Grace Chao from Hong Kong to participate in our discussions. Another younger woman from Chemical Bank in New York also joined us.

Texas Commerce allowed the vice president of its international department, Ping Ying Chou, to sit in on our meetings. Ping has been instrumental in our Aerobus planning ever since — and I am indebted to Texas Commerce for allowing Ping to give us a hand from time to time.

We not only spent time talking about the Aerobus design and financial matters, but we acted as first class Houston hosts for the entire week.

In anticipation of the Chinese arrival, I asked a good acquaintance of mine, Hunter Martin, Jr., to join me in laying plans and in conducting our deliberations. Hunter had retired from his oil industry career, and while he was working parttime still on a contract basis, he and I decided half of his time (or more) would be useful to Aerobus.

The week's activities included dinners and lunches of all description, separate visits to his and my homes, a barbecue at W. A. Smith's picturesque ranch an hour south of Houston (where we ate barbecue and presented each of the Chinese a Stetson cowboy hat), a night at the symphony in Jones Hall, an Astros baseball game in the Astrodome (followed by ice cream cones at a local ice cream outlet), a VIP visit to the Space Center, after which we had a special dinner at Gaido's Pelican Club, in Galveston, and plenty of free time for shopping at the Galleria in Houston.

We were pretty well exhausted as the visit grew to an end. We had champagne at my place the last night, at which our Chinese friends presented us with lovely gifts they had brought with them. Then we went to Maxim's for our sumptuous farewell dinner.

The next morning we gathered at the Chinese consulate on Montrose where, at 10 A.M., we had still more champagne — this time the Red Chinese version.

Under the aegis of the Consul General, we signed English and Chinese versions of a non-binding letter of intent. The paper memorialized our week of discussions and set the basis for our continued contracts and negotiations. In effect, both Aerobus and the ENFI people agreed that the two parties would proceed with the efforts to equip Chongqing with this 21st Century transit system.

The letter also recited my proposal that Aerobus create a new industry for China by allowing Chongqing to manufacture Aerobus systems, subject to its capacity to meet our engineering standards. My proposal has remained of primary interest to that city's representatives.

We are constantly reminded that we must have ample patience to do business with the Chinese. Various persons who have dealt with them confirm this, and the U. S. press speaks of it often. Our contacts so far reinforce that admonition. At the same time, we have shared many pleasurable moments.

The 1988 visit was just the beginning of a relationship that is still very much alive today.

For a period following the ENFI official visit, our contacts with the Chinese were intermittent. Ping Ying Chou traveled to China yearly on bank business and his wife, coincidentally, was born in Chongqing. From his acquaintanceship with Li Song (one of the engineers who became an expert on Aerobus technology) he knew that Chongqing was very much interested in our system.

In spite of these indications, it was apparent that their officials were not in a position to move quickly. Thus, I put my Aerobus plans pretty much on hold for awhile. Hunter Martin had left to pursue other interests fulltime, and I decided to exercise the necessary patience while waiting for further developments.

In 1991, I hired a young man, John Furnace, to assist in the office with my constant desire to develop markets for Aerobus. John, as a graduate of Houston Baptist University, had worked with a financial institution in Washington, D.C., and had returned to Houston, his home, with his family.

During the latter part of 1991, he mailed more than two hundred letters to a variety of possible Aerobus prospects. He also renewed our contact at Houston's Medical Center. Hunter Martin, in 1989, had made our first presentation to Bill Kuykendall, the assistant to the president of the Center.

We had studied the traffic congestion problems at the Medical Center, one of the world's largest, and had enlisted the aid of a Houston engineering firm to help refine our conclusions. That is, in time the Center would have inadequate parking facilities, both surface and garage parking. Daily more than 52,000 employees and staff go in and out of the Center's several hospitals at all hours. In addition, tens of thousands of visitors enter the sprawling complex daily to call on their ailing loved ones.

Information showed that most of these people, employees and visitors, arrived by automobile with only a small fraction using public transportation. On-site parking could only become a more severe problem as the surface parking lots were eliminated to make way for the construction of new medical buildings.

Aerobus proposed that its system be used to transport people from parking lots to be located at some distance from the Medical Center. Provisions could be made to run Aerobus through sheltered areas at the various buildings. During the nights, when employee-visitor traffic is lighter than daytime, we suggested that the Aerobus could be used to deliver supplies to various points within the Center from a central location.

We reopened our lines to the Medical Center, but the results were the same as before: disappointing. The problems will only get worse, however, and perhaps someday Aerobus will be considered to fill a very real hometown need.

The Chinese had reestablished their interest in September of 1991. We received a communication from ENFI (the engineering firm in Beijing) advising us of a new alignment for the Aerobus system in Chongqing. The new route differed from that considered by Vevey in its 1985 study. ENFI also queried us on the number of people an Aerobus system would be capable of moving one way each hour. (The answer depended on the number of vehicles. At the time, the system was designed to move hundreds.)

From the fall of '91 on, we have been working with both ENFI and Chongqing officials to develop a final plan for the Aerobus system to cross the Yangtze and Jailing Rivers. Visits to the U.S. as well as to China have been exchanged on several occasions.

Aerobus engineers, engaged by me on a consulting basis, have been to China twice to move ahead what has been a long and deliberate process of satisfying the Chinese on all of their questions. Along the way, we have undertaken a major redesign effort of Aerobus, which will enable the technology to meet codes and standards of any country in the world.

While preserving the unique, patented technology of the original Aerobus, the redesigned system provides an entirely new and modern appearance. Another significant development in the life of Aerobus, since I acquired it from the Swiss in 1987, arose as a result of new federal legislation signed into law in 1991. The bill, referred to as the Intermodal Surface Transportation Efficiency Act (ISTEA), provided for a number of new federal initiatives.

One of these was a pilot program to identify new technology for a suspended light rail system. Through a competitive process, the goal of ISTEA was to provide an opportunity for private enterprise and local government to obtain grant funding for innovative mass transit.

Aerobus learned of the competition from a contact John Furnace had made with the Milwaukee County supervisor, Larry Kenny. In 1991, Kenny had visited an exhibit booth Aerobus had leased at that year's convention of the American Public Transportation Association (APTA), which was held in Houston.

The Milwaukee supervisor's business card was in our files in the office among the cards of others who had visited the booth at the APTA convention. A letter to Larry Kenny was just one of the more than two hundred that John mailed out that year.

An exchange of letters led to a phone call that ignited a deeper interest in Aerobus on the part of the county official. The upshot of this routine contact was that Milwaukee County selected Aerobus technology as the one to be used in entering the ISTEA pilot program.

Milwaukee County plans to install an Aerobus system to serve the needs of its growing Regional Medical Complex. The officials considered Aerobus as ideal to assist in a controlled growth of the complex; it would ease traffic congestion and not contribute to increased air pollution.

It strikes me as ironic that while making no headway in my hometown of Houston, with our own world renowned Medical Center, the officials in Milwaukee County embraced the capabilities of Aerobus. This is what we believe it can do: move more people, over more obstacles, with more ease and speed and safety, less pollution, and less upkeep than any other such systems of mass transportation. And do it all, in the long term, with more economy.

In my early conversations with Milwaukee County representatives, I told them what a Houston doctor had told me. His office is less than a mile from the Texas Medical Center. On the day he was describing to me, he said he had a patient in an emergency room of one of the hospitals. In trying to hurry to the patient, he said he was prevented from arriving due to traffic gridlock in and around the Center.

Upon hearing the story, the Milwaukee people said they had observed the traffic tieups in Houston and that it was exactly the kind of congestion they wanted to avoid by using Aerobus. Milwaukee's planning includes: in the event of an emergency at its Medical Complex, a program of restricting employees access except by riding Aerobus from remote parking lots.

The ISTEA pilot program provided for a competition to be entered into by local governments to earn a grant to develop a new transit technology. Three of the entrants utilized the Aerobus technology. In addition to Milwaukee County, Big Bear Lake and

Palm Desert, both in California, formed a "partnership" with Aerobus for submitting proposals.

The Federal Transit Administration first selected seven of the original seventeen entrants for detailed discussions. Then, there were three finalists chosen from the first seven — Montgomery County, Maryland; Oakland, California and Milwaukee County! Thus, the promise of Aerobus technology became recognized by the FTA.

The three finalists then split an award of one million dollars, matched in part by local funds, to be used for a more detailed engineering submittal.

In 1994, the FTA began its evaluation of the proposals. Time was not of the essence, as reflected in the fact that Congress has not yet funded the $30 Million grant. Nevertheless, the outcome of the competition to date highlights the faith all of us place in this concept. We especially appreciate the dedication of Larry Kenny and others in Milwaukee County.

In preparing the proposal for the federal competition, it was necessary for Aerobus to bring on board persons with transit engineering background. Again, I consulted with Wolfgang Bamberg, who recommended a former FTA executive, George Pastor.

A man then in his middle sixties, Pastor is a native of Hungary. A resident of Falls Church, Virginia, fifteen minutes from the White House, he holds a bachelor's degree and a masters in electrical engineering from Columbia University and the University of Southern California, respectively. Since 1971, he has served in various executive management positions in industry and government in the field of urban transportation. His federal tenure included being associate adminstrator of the Urban Mass Transit Administration (UMTA is the predecessor of today's Federal Transit Administration.) Among other private industry assignments, he worked at the Lockheed Missile Systems Division and subsequently at Ford Aerospace. He contributed greatly to NASA's development of our space program, thus he was no stranger to the Houston scene.

An inveterate talker, my visits with him have contributed immeasurably to my deeper appreciation of the engineering intricacies involved in updating the Aerobus technology.

As an independent consultant, Pastor, along with John Furnace's support, guided the preparation of our initial submission on the ISTEA competition.

When Milwaukee County was selected as a finalist, faced with submitting a much more detailed "second level" proposal, Pastor advised me that Aerobus required additional engineering expertise. Much to his credit, he realized that his electrical engineering degrees and transit industry experience did not qualify him as a top rate mechanical engineer, whose talents were required for the more detailed workup.

Pastor called on a former associate he had worked with, and supervised, in private industry — Don Sullivan, who lived in the Los Angeles area and had a fulltime job in the transit industry. But by working at night and during the weekends, he assured me he could meet the needs of Aerobus. Thus, he also joined our fledgling Aerobus "team" as a consultant. Sullivan then contacted other engineers with whom he had worked, primarily Ben Lamoreaux of Cedar City, Utah, to assist him.

While I recognized that these three men, together with additional support engineers, collectively represented more than one hundred fifty years of transit industry engineering and management experience, it occurred to me that we should bring on board a company in Switzerland intimately acquainted with our product. That firm, APCO Technologies S.A., is headed by André Pugin, our old friend who had negotiated on behalf of Vevey Engineering when I purchased Aerobus.

I knew the Chinese held in high respect the expertise of the Swiss with regard to cable technolgoy. So I entered into a contract with Pugin's company to design certain aspects of the new Aerobus (the bogie, chassis and articulation joint.) This was all in connection with the federal competition. I had complete confidence in André and his people. Having him assisting us provided me with considerable comfort of mind.

I later awarded to APCO the design contract of the guideway portion of the Aerobus system — that is, the track of elevated "roadway" along which the vehicle would run.

At the same time, it became necessary to identify an engineering firm to redesign the Aerobus car body. The original Aerobus was never intended to move ten thousand passengers or more per hour in the same direction, but that was what the Chinese were now expecting. Pastor and Sullivan recommended turning to a firm in Salt Lake City — (IDI) Intermountain Design, Inc. Aerobus signed a contract with IDI to redesign the Aerobus carbody.

All of these various consultants, in California, Utah, Virginia and Switzerland, comprise the current Aerobus family.

In February of 1994, Hunter Martin rejoined me. I needed him as president of Aerobus to provide fulltime, day to day attention to the reports being received from the various consultants, and most importantly to help control costs.

Barry Goodman, former head of Houston's Metro system, also had become a valuable consultant to me. He was instrumental in interesting the Palm Desert City Council in Aerobus, and directed the preparation by that city of its proposal in the ISTEA competition. He and I remain in contact.

Interest in Aerobus springs from most unexpected sources. For example, the city of Budapest, Hungary was planning a World's Fair. Transit people from that beautiful Eastern European capital attended in October, 1992, the convention of the American Public Transit Association in New Orleans. John Furnace manned an Aerobus booth at the gathering and the Budapest people became interested in using the system at their World's Fair.

It would have been an ideal showcase. George Pastor, while on a trip to Europe, visited in Budapest and kept the interest there stirring. In the end, however, and most regrettably, the timetable was too short and the negotiations were discontinued.

We realize every day that what Aerobus needs most is a demonstration test facility to prove on the ground what our redesign effort shows analytically. That is, that the updated technology of Aerobus offers to the world a cost-competitive mode of transportation that is attractive, quiet, pollution-free and least disruptive to ground conditions of the areas where it is installed. The test facility, to be located in the Houston area, is very much on our agenda of things to do in the development of the new Aerobus.

In the meantime, Aerobus has undertaken a more spirited marketing program throughout the United States. Interestingly, Big Bear Lake invited Aerobus to compete in a feasibility study to select a preferred transit technology to serve this Southern California summer-winter resort area.

Looking back at my long experience with this venture, I sometimes ask: has it been worthwhile? The answer is that it has been — and I am convinced that we are approaching the stage when all our efforts will bear fruit. Aerobus by Parks has not been without its problems, but solving problems (and in turn winning a fair number of lawsuits) is how I have spent most of my life.

If Thomas Edison had abandoned the light bulb after his first fifty or so failures, we might still be reading today by candle or gaslight. It is not in my nature to accept defeat, and so, ten years after we began, this quest continues.

While I may, in the twilight of my life, never see Aerobus in operation, I am convinced that this unique technology offers outstanding transit possibilities for the 21st Century.

Chapter 8

Once There Were
Green Fields

THE LATE JIMMY DEMARET, bon vivant and phi-
losopher, once said that there were two things you
could enjoy without being good at them: golf and sex.

It has been my policy to avoid subjects I am not
qualified to discuss, but I can tell you that few games
will fulfill and humble you the way golf does. The
greatest charm of the sport is obvious: a golf course is
a beautiful place to be. You can't say the same about a
basketball court, a baseball diamond or a football field.

Golf gets you closest to nature, among the trees,
lush green grass, white sands and beds of flowers. Of
course, some players fail to appreciate this benefit, and
are satisfied if they can tell the difference between Ber-
muda grass and poison ivy.

Of course, the game can test and torment you.
When Greg Norman blew a seven-stroke lead on the
final round of the 1996 Masters, duffers all over

America said, "I can feel his pain." As you may or may not have noted, golf spelled backwards is flog.

I didn't take up the game until I returned from service after World War II, meaning that I was still able to play for fifty years.

As a boy, I was fortunate to attend a small high school, where I took part in four sports, baseball, basketball, track and football. At Rice, I went out for football, but discovered quickly that I didn't have enough time to keep up with my classes, hold down a job and practice for the team.

As I worked my way through school and later the courts, bowling and tennis became my forms of recreation. I played tennis at most of the public courts and before I went in the service, when I wanted to get in shape, I joined the Turnavine Club. When I was an intelligence officer in Italy, I had to answer a question about this membership. It came up in my security background check — at one time the Turnavine had been a German social club.

Nevertheless, I played a lot of tennis on week ends, and the day before I enlisted I set my personal record of one hundred games in one day.

When I returned home after the war, my doctor advised me to take up a less strenuous sport and he suggested golf. So I called on the coach of the Rice golf team, Jim Deal, and took five lessons from him. When I finished, I bought the finest set of golf clubs on the market. I told Jim I wanted to blame myself for any mistakes I made and not the clubs.

The first club I joined was Lakeside Country

Club and soon I was addicted to the game. Later, I became a member at Champions, the club developed by Demaret and Jackie Burke, Jr. After some years there, I left and was one of the founders of Lochinvar, a men's only course. I served on the board of directors and was elected captain of the club, a title I continue to hold to this day.

By the early 1960's, I had concluded that a man should be able to make a living in ten months and take two off to travel and play golf. And for years I have done just that.

A friend of mine was a member of the El Dorado Country Club in Indian Wells, in Palm Springs, and he told me he thought I would enjoy playing the course there. He arranged for me to get a month's guest pass and he was right. I liked the course, and Mrs. Parks and I spent a month in Palm Springs the next two winters.

The third year, 1962, my friend invited me to join and I did, paying $700 for my membership. Today a membership at El Dorado sells for $60,000 and I've had mine for over thirty years. We began to go to California frequently and spent several months.

Some ten years ago, we joined the Vintage Club, in the desert, in the shade of the Santa Rosa Mountains. We built a condo close to the clubhouse, then decided we would prefer a house. We bought the largest lot ever plotted at the Vintage, nine-tenths of an acre, and built a home on Hummingbird Lane, which we still own.

The first time I ever shot my age was on the Vintage course. Playing in a club tournament, I shot a 76 — I was 77 years old at the time — winning a trophy in the process. There were two low balls and I scored on sixteen of the eighteen holes. From that time on, until I had to give up golf because of a balance problem, I shot my age occasionally.

An inner ear disturbance forced me to give up the game in my early eighties, but I have a lifetime of memories. I enjoyed playing at Shady Oaks Country Club in Fort Worth, where I became acquainted with Ben Hogan. We became friends, and on my office wall hangs a photograph of Hogan's great shot to win the 1950 U. S. Open at the Merion Golf Course, at Ardmore, Pa. The inscription on the photo reads: "To a pal of mine. Ben Hogan."

There will be few of these found in anyone's lifetime. Hogan has been among the most private of our sports heroes. He avoided the camera and crowds.

In my opinion, there was never a greater striker of the ball than Ben Hogan. Among those who agreed with me was Jimmy Demaret, who was asked this question: if you could enter all of history's best golfers, in their prime, in one tournament, who would win?

"Oh, I think Ben Hogan," he said, "is an easy answer. Ben had every shot in the bag. He was the kind of guy who could isolate himself from everything but knocking the ball in the cup. I think Arnold Palmer is the most radiant personality the game has ever known. But the greatest golfer, tee to green and through the green, would be Hogan. He was great under the worst kind of pressure."

After he cured the duck hook that he had early on, and became able to work the ball, Hogan could place his shots better than any man I have ever read about or watched. One could go on for pages, extolling the virtues of this man and the many things he taught me, and others, about golf and life.

As these words are written, Hogan has been in ill health. I used to call him on his birthday and we talked back and forth. Now I call his wife and when he feels able to talk, she hands him the phone for a few, precious minutes.

I had more than my fair share of unique moments in golf. Once, when I was in my home at The Vintage, a friend called and said he had arranged a golf game and hoped I could join them. The match was going to be played at a nearby course financed with money from the Teamsters' Union in Alaska.

That fact had no significance until I was told that my friend and I would be playing the club pro and his guest. When we joined them, it turned out that the guest was Jimmy Hoffa, the dominant figure in the labor movement at that time and one of history's most famous missing persons.

My friend had done some business with the Teamsters and I believe to this day, although I can't prove it, that he deliberately hit a ball into the lake so that we lost the match.

The interesting part of the story is that everyone in the U. S. government seemed to be looking for Mr. Hoffa at the time we were enjoying a sunny day in the desert, playing a round of golf. Later, no one was able to find Jimmy Hoffa. According to the most persistent rumor, his body is buried under the end zone at The Meadowlands, the field where the New York Giants and Jets play their home games.

I believe there were three factors that lifted golf out of the category of an elite country club game and made the PGA tour a multi-million dollar enterprise. They are: Dwight Eisenhower, Arnold Palmer and television.

The charisma of Palmer and the power of television need no elaboration. But Eisenhower gave golf a boost that can't be measured when he had a putting green installed on the White House lawn. He visited Augusta as often as he could, and his escape to the links was a sort of Papal blessing for any businessman who wanted to follow.

It happened that the builder of the El Dorado Country Club was among those grateful for the exposure Ike gave the game, and he leased a cottage to him for a dollar a year. I would see Eisenhower in the locker room from time to time, and enjoyed our brief conversations, nearly always in the presence of others.

One day, I heard the builder ask how he the former president was enjoying his cottage. He said, fine, but it had certain inconveniences. There was no room for the Secret Service agents, who were still assigned to guarding him, to change their clothes or store their weapons.

The builder said that was no problem, and he built a larger home for the Eisenhowers on the 11th fairway. This cottage had separate quarters for the Secret

Service agents. My wife would bump into Mamie Eisenhower at the Main Chance Spa in Phoenix.

Ike would take a short lesson almost every morning from one of the lady instructors. He was well received by everyone at the club. I will always treasure those rare moments when I was in his company.

Golf is truly a sport of cabbages and kings. Claude Harmon, one of the finest teachers the game has known and a longtime friend of mine, once asked if I would like to play in the King's Tournament in Morocco. In short order, Mrs. Parks and I joined Claude and his wife and flew to Morocco, a few miles from Spain, across the Strait of Gibraltar. The country's largest and best known city is Casablanca, the setting for a classic movie of the same name.

Claude had been the king's golf coach for many years, until he finally turned the job over to his oldest son, Butch, whose recent clients include Greg Norman and Tiger Woods.

I asked Claude why he made the switch. He said when the king started telling him how to play golf, he thought it was time for a new teacher.

Still, Claude went to his tournament and the king always furnished him with a chauffeur and limousine, paid all his expenses and gave him a fine set of silver when he left.

That year the king did not attend the festivities because an attempt had been made on his life. In spite of his absence, we were wined and dined royally, and entertained by belly dancers. But the best perk of all was the limo. The other pros and amateurs were transported by a bus. We rode with Claude and his wife in the limo, and even when others had to park blocks away we were given door to door service.

I gave high grades to both the trip and the tournament. On our way home I raised the idea of Claude coming to Lochinvar as the teaching pro. It was a slightly different kind of employment when we got the terms worked out. He would give free instruction to the members and guests, but no scheduled lessons. At the present time, his son, Butch, is the pro at Lochinvar.

Sometimes, it isn't what you learn while playing golf that matters. It's what you learn in the locker room or on the practice tee that stays with you.

I met Bart Starr, the hall of fame quarterback for the Green Bay Packers, at an invitational tournament at The Vintage, and got to ask him a question that had been on my mind for quite awhile.

I told him I had been watching on TV the championship game between the Packers and the Dallas Cowboys in 1967, in Green Bay, that became known as the Ice Bowl. The temperature that day was so cold that when the officials tried to blow their whistles, they tore the skin off their lips.

I was watching on television as the Packers, trailing by 17-14, moved down the field, racing the clock, the freezing cold and the icy footing. Snow was piled high in banks on the sidelines. The Packers had the ball on the one-yard line with a few seconds left on the clock, enough time to attempt a tying field goal or one play to win or lose it all.

I made a bet that the Packers would run the ball over center to win the game. I told Starr all I wanted to

261

know was, "What did he and Vince Lombardi say to one another during the timeout?"

Starr laughed and said, "You really want to know?"

He said Lombardi asked what play he wanted to call and Bart told him. The coach nodded and said, "Hurry up and get the damned thing over with — I'm freezing to death."

Starr went back onto the field, called the play, followed the block of Jerry Kramer and knifed inside the center to score, winning the game and sending the Packers on to the Super Bowl.

As I sit here making a few correction in the book, I have a reflection of yesterday's tournament in which Tiger Woods won his second professional tournament since turning pro and has won approximately three-quarters of a million dollars since he turned pro. I will make a prediction to all of you that read this book that are lovers of golf, that Tiger, in his lifetime, will surpass all of the records that have ever been made by all who have ever played the game.

I am reminded of what Hogan said when we were sitting around the table about what the future held for golf. Someone remarked that the youngsters might not be as good as some of the oldtimers. Hogan replied: "We have failed if this happens because it is our duty and purpose to teach others how to improve the game". I think Tiger will make Hogan's remarks a truism!

Chapter 9

Grape Expectations:
Wining and Dining

"A Jug of Wine, a Loaf of Bread — and Thou
Beside me singing in the Wilderness —"
       — The Rubiyat of Omar Khayyam.

AT THE TIME I entered the military, in late 1942, I was a whiskey drinker, but not to excess, partial to bourbon and scotch. Through a series of benign circumstances, already described, I helped establish an enlisted man's club in Italy and also built up a rather nice private collection.

During the war, whiskey became a form of currency and you used it to barter for other goods and favors and even military supplies.

When whiskey grew scarce, I began to drink Italian wines. When I went out on investigations, I got in the habit of stopping to have lunch and a glass of wine. I reached a point where I liked wine at least as well as whiskey.

When I came back from the war, my lifestyle changed in two ways from what it had been before: I gave up tennis for golf and started drinking wine, almost exclusively.

As a kind of personal test, I will take some scotch with water, just to see if the taste brings back any memories, or longings, but it simply does not exhilarate me like a glass of fine wine.

I attended my first Escoffier meeting at the Houston Club over forty years ago and it was there that I began to cultivate my taste in wines. I have not missed a meeting since, if I was in town.

As pleasures do, this interest turned into both a hobby and a quest. On many of the thirty or so trips Mrs. Parks and I have made to Europe, wherever we stopped we tried the wines — all kinds, German, French, Italian, Spanish.

I put in a cellar when we lived on Del Monte, and in the Houston Club, where the racks are south of the Azalea Room. I was instructed by the members to get the club to do so because there had been problems with the wines. I told the managers to build some racks, put the wine in and compare the empty bottles against their checks. If they did not have empty bottles to match, then somebody was stealing the wine.

Little by little, I educated myself. I can remember at the Escoffier dinners, you could count the glasses and tell how many different kinds of wines we were going to have. The men in Escoffier, most of whom were foreign born, with great knowledge of food and wine, taught me by their comments and by answering my questions. I began to read books about wine.

As time went on, it was suggested that I take over the Wine Commitee at the Escoffier, a position I held for many years. Finally, I stepped aside in favor of others who, in my opinion, were more knowledgeable. By now everyone had heard all of my stories, although on occasion I will still give the history on the life of Escoffier and his home, which is now a museum where I have visited on several occasions.

The earliest references to wine appear in the picture writings of the ancient Egyptians and Babylonians, five thousand years ago.

In a comparison between wine and whiskey, it is fairly easy to describe the effects of scotch or bourbon in that you get a quick stimulation and then it begins to taper off. The more you drink, the more likely you are to get intoxicated. With a good bottle of wine, the effect is quite different. First, you have prepared yourself for the enjoyment of the wine. I learned from others to order in a sequence different than most. I order my wine first and then I order food that is compatible with the wine. If I select a champagne, I taste it. Champagne will go with anything.

If I order a bottle of Montrachet de la Guiche, which is one of the finest and most expensive wines in the world, sometimes running two thousand dollars a case, wholesale, I will have a sip to determine if it is good, then a glass. Before I take a drink, I pause to appreciate the color and, with champagne, the bubbles. The sip has an exhilarating effect and a departure effect which are entirely unlike the sensations you get from whiskey. It is what makes you enjoy this particular wine more.

It is a pleasant feeling, rather than a feeling of

shock to your system. A long time ago, I learned that taste is the robber sense. It steals from other senses. You are only able to taste sweet, sour, salt and bitter. Those taste buds are on different parts of your tongue. Taste steals from the sense of smell and from the sense of sight.

A good way for you to test this yourself is to take a day when you have a bad cold, and eat something highly seasoned or wine that has a highly distinct flavor. You will find them bland. With a cold, you lack a sense of smell and food that is not attractive looking won't taste as good.

At this time, I have a wine cellar in my home at The Huntingdon, and one in my home at The Vintage in Indian Wells, California. I lean to the particularly good white burgundy wine. My favorite is Montrachet de la Guiche, although there are many others that qualify as great.

In California, they had great vineyards where the wine was not outstanding because it was grown on desert soil and was irrigated. It was too bland, but they could and did make large quantities of it. Now they all recognize their problem with the soil and irrigation and most of the good wines from California come from the Napa Valley.

As far as food (and hotels) are concerned, they are graded by the Michelin Guide, which is published annually. The 1994 edition lists five three-star restaurants (the highest rating) in Paris, and considerably more two-star establishments and still more that rated one star.

Our selection of the finest place to eat, in all our

travels, is the Taillevent, owned by Mr. Vrinat, and they in turn have the finest wine cellar in Paris and exemplary food. The ambience is not as strong as some other restaurants, but when you put the wine, food and service together it stands without peer in our minds.

For many years, Mrs. Parks and I spent a month in France, primarily in the wine region during the gathering of the grapes. I had opportunities to visit many of the famous vineyards, and watch as they would prepare the wines after the grapes were picked. Over time, I expanded my knowledge of the fine wines of the world, German, Italian, French and American. My favorite red is one of the regal French wines, that is, Lafitte Mouton Margaux Rothschild.

If not the most elegant or the most expensive, by far the most impressive menu I have discovered is that of the Bern's Steak House, in Tampa, Florida.

The menu features over one thousand items on the dessert menu, including drinks. In the dessert room, there are booths that seat either two, four, six, eight, ten or twelve guests.

When I attended a Super Bowl game in Tampa, with 50-yard line seats provided by some political friends, there were twelve or fourteen people in our party. Someone in the group called the Bern's Steak House and they said they were all sold out and couldn't seat us.

I told them to let me see if I could pull any strings. I called the owner at his farm, and he offered to check and call us back. He did, and said they would take care of us. He had them put a table in the middle of the floor.

The Bern's Steak House has more wine than any other private cellar in the United States, perhaps the world, with the possible exception of the large vineyards. So many people come in by limousine that the limo company made the restaurant their headquarters. You can order one from your table.

If I was to know that I would be condemned to die and would have one last meal, I would take a bottle of Roederer Cristal Champagne, properly chilled and served, followed by a bouillabaisse soup, with a Montrachet de la Guiche. Following that I would choose dover sole or sea bass sauteed meniere, then placed to one side on a hot skillet and served with appropriate vegetables.

The dessert would almost take care of itself after that meal, but I would order a cognac. As I no longer smoke, there would be no cigars. Sorry about that, but it's my menu.

LAGNIAPPE: Armagnac always bears a vintage date, but not every wine does. Only recently, a change in French law now permits a vintage date on all wines. For port, the best years are considered 1963 through 1970. For those who enjoy trivia, Calvados is applejack made from Norman apples.

In the spring of 1996, I donated much of my wine cellar to the University of Houston's Hotel School, on the campus. The collection was appraised at $75,000 and a matching grant was approved by the Board of Regents.

I am especially honored that this addition will be known as the Fred Parks Wine Cellar.

REFLECTIONS ON GOOD TASTE

With my compliments to:

Erik Worscheh, my role model and mentor in the world of wine and food.

Denman Moody, my friend and connoisseur of fine wines.

Le Comite Permanent of Le Chapitre de Houston of Les Amis d'Escoffier, composed of: Joe Mannke, president; Erik Worscheh, Horst Manhard, Walter Kayser, James deGeorge, Willard (Red) Steger, Fritz Girscher, Bernard van Mourik, Jack Sorcic, Lenoir Josey, Bernard Urban, Henry Audley and myself. Several of these eminent men are foreign born chefs. All are experts in food and wine and all the pleasure that accompany the serving of them.

✳✳ The Committee of Nine, for more than thirty years, comprised of well known Houston food and beverage personalities. The group is looked upon as the city's most distinguished "gastronomic" committee, which holds luncheons and dinners throughout the year with individual members acting as host. I am the only member with no formal food or beverage training. Present committee members are: "Uppy" Upshaw, Steger, Manhard, Mannke, Walter Asche, van Mourik, Worsceh and myself.

✳✳ Michael Humphrey and his partners conceived, formed and constructed The Vintage Club in Indian Wells, California, one of the most fabulous clubs in the world.

✳✳ Peter Malch, formerly with the El Dorado

269

Country Club, and the present executive chef, Ulrich Ludwig, are masters of the preparation and serving of fine food and wine. Both acquired their skills from living in the "Old Country." Their presence makes the U. S. a better place.

** A void of long standing finally has been ended with the opening in January, of 1996, of the Givenchy Hotel and Spa in Palm Springs, with its impeccable standards of legendary fashion and fragrances, all on a fourteen-acre domain with ninety-eight luxurious accomodations.

** Freeman Money, now at Lochinvar, has graciously made life more pleasant for more people in Houston than any other living person in the city.

** Paul Bruggermans and Chef Michael Despras for adding the new Le St. Germain restaurant in Indian Wells to their famous Le Vallauris, the five-star winning restaurant in Palm Springs.

** Ely Callaway, whom I have known from the El Dorado and Vintage Clubs, for his Midas touch in converting any enterprise he conceives into gold.

** Jack P. Hennessy and his wife, Shirley, whose bountiful hospitality in the wine country of both California and France, will forever be appreciated by Mrs. Parks and me.

EPILOGUE

REFLECTIONS

Having distilled in these pages nearly a century of living, I find it fitting to close with a compilation — of people whose paths I crossed, whose lives touched mine, and mine theirs:

WITH JUSTICE FOR ALL

✱✱ My comment to a Territorial Judge in Alaska, before it became a state, about when to set my case for trial: "Judge, you should take judicial notice that I live in Texas. My blood is thin and, therefore, you should set the case in the summertime." And he agreed. My local counsel in the case, became the state of Alaska's first governor.

✱✱ In a joint custody case, I represented the mother and the father, a lawyer, represented himself. Both were Jewish. I called the mother's rabbi to testify about her fitness for custody, in that she was leaving the state of Texas. On cross-examination, the husband said: "Rabbi, you have testified about my wife's qualifications. Now, you are my rabbi, also. Would you testify about my qualifications as to the custody of my children?" The rabbi replied: "I'd rather not say."

✱✱ Tom Alexander: all that needs to be said is my nickname for him: the Mighty Tom Alexander!

✱✱ Lloyd Barber, a former FBI agent and later a private investigator, collected evidence for me over the years and was so essential to my successful practice of law. In addition, he produced and protected witnesses for my trials.

** William Bonham was licensed to practice law in 1954, and instead became a tennis player. Later, he was associated with a well known sports agent, Mark McCormack, who at one time represented Arnold Palmer, Jack Nicklaus, Gary Player and a number of tennis professionals. One day, Bill came to me for a job because his wife had given him an ultimatum: continue being a sports agent and get a divorce, or quit and practice law. He started at a beginning lawyer's salary and now is the head of a well seasoned law firm that at one time had thirty-five lawyers. In 1991, Bill won the world tennis championship, in Australia, for men sixty years and older.

** Sloan Blair, many times my associate in law, who is also my personal lawyer. His first draft of a brief is like the finished product of most lawyers.

** The Bracewell "Clan" was among the first to befriend me when I began my practice of law, starting with father Jim. His two fine sons, Searcy and Fentress, built one of Houston's most prestigious law firms.

** Judge Roy Campbell smoked Bull Durham cigarettes from the bench. On one occasion, I had a witness on the stand and asked if he he had brought certain documents. He said, no, and he did not intend to produce the papers.

Judge Campbell rolled and lit his cigarette and asked the witness to repeat himself. When he did, the judge asked how long it would take to get the papers "if he wanted to get them.". The witness said two hours. Judge Campbell called the sheriff. He told him to take a good look at the witness because, if he was not back in court with the papers in two hours, the sheriff was to pick him up and slap him in Hill's jail at the foot of Capitol Street.

** I feel entitled to take some credit for the marriage of George Cire and his lovely Peggy. When George was my top associate, he began to show up on Mondays in a tired condition. After investigating, I learned that he was courting Peggy, who lived in Paris, Texas. I gave him two alternatives: either get a girlfriend closer to home or marry Peggy. He made the right choice.

** Dick DeGuerin gets my vote as the top criminal lawyer in the United States, even surpassing F. Lee (Flea) Bailey.

** Donn Fullenweider has achieved recognition as one of the top lawyers in his field.

** Gibson Gayle, of Fulbright & Jaworski, has been a true friend and one of Houston's outstanding citizens.

** Diego Giordano, a fine Ft. Worth attorney, who has helped me tread the path of justice in Ecuador.

** Bob Hudson, a very able, conservative lawyer and devoted associate, who is always available when I need him.

** Joe Jamail received the largest legal fee in the history of U. S. jurisprudence, after representing Pennzoil in its successful suit against Texaco. Joe was a young boy sacking groceries in his family's store when I first knew him. While there, he refined a personal trait that later served him well: he never met a stranger and this, in lawyer's parlance, enabled him to "work a crowd." At my suggestion, he worked almost a year in the district attorney's office, where the pressures of the environment taught him how to take charge of a courtroom — something he used while working in my office, before he emerged on his own to become one of the leading trial attorneys in America.

** Charles Oakley came to me as an associate in a time of my need to help reduce a horrendous backlog of cases, which he was very well qualified to handle.

** Ruby Sondock, who worked for me for years, went on to become a domestic relations judge, later a fine district court judge and served with distinction on the Texas Supreme Court.

** I achieved an unusual *adoption by estoppel* of a girl whose foster parents had died before completing their final adoption. The girl had lived in their house for a number of years during which the parents had on numerous occasions stated their intentions to adopt her. When heirs of the couple intervened to "grab" the assets from the "parents," I was able to impose an "adoption by estoppel" so that the young lady was able to prevail over the others in their claim of the assets.

ALL IN THE FAMILY

** My wife, Mabel Parks, was the first elected president of the Women's Auxiliary of Texas Children's Hospital in Houston. I wrote their constitution, which has remained unchanged for thirty years.

** Mark Stauffer, grandson, has two talents, as an illustrator and musician.

** Kristian Stauffer, granddaughter, is a beautiful and vivacious young lady.

** Ann Stallings, granddaughter, is a graduate of the University of Texas, and recently completed a course with highest honors in Minnesota. Her husband, Dennis, is a par golfer.

DEAR HEARTS AND GENTLE PEOPLE

** Dr. Denton Cooley, better known as "Fast Blade," hung seven by-

273

passes on me — six on my heart and one on my leg — and Dena, his associate, without whom he could not function.

** Fayez Sarofim, financial wizard and a firm believer in equities, has been a helping hand for years.

** Ping Ying Chou, America's finest Far East expert.

** Ann Davis Sheptak, after ten years of being my personal secretary and bookkeeper, wanted a career change. I let her work parttime so she could get her license as a CPA, after which she became a financial counselor.

** Jane Love, my first and longtime trusted private secretary, would take a leave to have her children. When she finally withdrew from the office, I could never convince her to return. She later passed away from a malady that she never disclosed to me.

** Johnny Price, now deceased, handled my tax returns in an exemplary manner for many years.

** The late Joan Robinson Hill, whose death was so tragic, is still remembered as an equestrian par excellence.

** G. P. Pearson has been a longtime, steadfast friend with a lovely daughter and two successful sons.

** Adelaide Englebrecht is the fair-minded manager of The Huntingdon, where I live. She has shown her executive capabilities in weathering many of the cross-currents among the homeowners of that lively building. Her burden is to say "no" to any unreasonable requests from the owners and yet keep The Huntingdon running smoothly.

THE ONE THAT GOT AWAY

I chased a rainbow for nearly ten years. The name of the rainbow is Ecuador, and I tried mightily to track it to the end.

For thirty years before I got involved, companies had competed to gain the rights to explore for huge natural gas reserves in the Gulf of Guayaquil.

South America has always been a magnet for oilmen, who, by definition, are endowed with a sense of adventure. I looked at the developments in Caracas, Venezuela, and always reasoned: "What if one could find ten Caracases in all of South America — just think what you would have."

So I was more than casually interested when a Dallas oil operator named Cloyce Box, with one of his engineers, appeared in my office. Box, who had a strong track record, said he had "checked me out." He concluded that I had the contacts, and the tenacity, to take advantage of an international oil and gas opportunity in Ecuador. The natural gas reserves alone ran into the trillions of cubic feet.

By the time they left that day in 1978, I was hooked.

The history of American wildcatting in Ecuador was a decades-long tale of millions invested, and lost, of a government overthrown by a military junta, of contracts canceled and failed lawsuits.

By 1968, Ecuador had granted a petroleum concession to eight companies led by Ada Oil, owned by Houston's Bud Adams. Nine wells and $30 Million dollars later, the military government refused to renew a contract with the consortium. Instead, it awarded new rights to the U.S. — based Northwest Energy.

Ada filed a lawsuit against Northwest and assigned its interest to a subsidiary one of the consortium members. When the lawsuit was dismissed, I stepped in and acquired the rights in May of 1981, and folded them into Fred Parks, Inc.

I found that I had not only taken possession of a mountain of geological data, and documents relating to previous explorations. I had also inherited an office with a secretary in Quito, contracts with consultants and even a chauffeur (who became one of my employees.)

But this was to be a tangled web of efforts that went nowhere. Negotiations were always at the mercy of Ecuador's politics. We did succeed in developing good relations with some of the country's ministers, but these efforts were undermined by our domestic partners, who wilted along the way, and French partners, who waffled and stalled. There were endless exchanges of letters and telegrams, meetings in Paris, Houston, New York and Ecuador.

What followed was close to ten years of agreements not quite sealed, of delays and deception. Trying to figure out the various positions was like trying to lift a bale of hay with no handles. It came apart in your arms. By the summer of 1989, the French company that had assumed the role of managing partner had withdrawn. The patience of Ecuador's oil and gas authorities had been exhausted. Efforts to find new investors were unsuccessful. My Guayaquil venture had drawn to a slow and painful conclusion.

I recovered none of the expenses that had been incurred, but I have never surrendered any of my legal options. There were no silver linings, and not much in the way of consolation, except to count Ecuador as another learning experience; however, I still have a pending claim in Ecuador.

REFLECTIONS ON OTHER ROADS TAKEN

✻✻ Seeing the Berlin Wall and the graveyard, where those who had tried to escape and failed were buried. And, later, walking through the Brandenberg Gate, after the Wall came tumbling down.

** A visit to Egypt, where I went into the Pyramids, rode a camel and took a trip down the Nile River.

** The Wailing Wall in Jerusalem, and an escorted trip by the Israelis to the Golan Heights. Visiting a Kibbutz, where both the young men and women (Israel's "Minute Men") had been trained for war.

While in Israel, a Scotsman gave me a tour through the local courts and explained that this young nation had lacked legal precedents on which to build the nation's legal system. Upon returning to the U.S., I had delivered to him a multi-year subscription to the *University of Texas Law Review*.

REFLECTIONS FROM THE FAIRWAY

As the late Harvey Penick put it, if you love golf you're my friend:

** Jack Lee, who played quarterback for Houston and Denver, among other teams, and along with myself and others was one of the founding members of Lochinvar.

** John Brodie, one of the best golfers ever to play pro football. Had a fine career with the 49ers and when his passing days were over he joined the senior PGA Tour. We met on a golf course and started a friendship that turned into a lawyer-client relationship, when I solved a legal problem for John.

** Sparky Hauch, former board director of The Vintage, and Paul Lemcke, director of golf, who have contributed immeasurely to my enjoyment of the club.

** Roland E. Casati, of Lake Forest, Illinois, along with his wife, among my golfing buddies at The Vintage.

** The Harmon Family — the world's finest golf teaching family. When the patriarch, Claude, was terminally ill and depressed, I told him he could not die to which he asked: "Why can't I die."

I then told him why: "Because he was the only man with a green coat (the symbol of winning the Masters) that I could beat."

My joking around led Claude to get out his clubs and begin practicing. For a year, he and I played as partners at Lochinvar and never lost.

His four sons have always been kind enough to say that I had helped extend their father's life.

FEELINGS

I have known:

** The satisfaction of a job well done, when, on July 12, 1937, I was awarded my law degree from South Texas College and could then commence my practice of law.

276

** The disappointment of not becoming a Marine in World War II, being unable to pass the physical due to orthodontic problems.

** The thrill of seeing Dicky Maegle of Rice awarded a touchdown in the Cotton Bowl, although he never crossed the goal. On New Year's Day of 1954, Dicky was credited with a 95-yard scoring run after an Alabama player, Tommy Lewis, jumped off the bench to make the tackle.

** The shock and surprise of hearing William A. Smith announce to the regulars who met for coffee each morning that he had been a member of the CIA. He had turned it down once, then received a telephone call from President Lyndon Johnson. Smith said he did not want to be involved. The president replied: "You have a choice. You can join, or you will be drafted on Monday." So he accepted. Obviously, all of us in the regular morning coffee "club" had been under surveillance for years without knowing it. Question: Had our civil rights been violated?

** Skepticism as my first reaction to the U-2 plane on exhibit in Moscow. I did not believe it had been shot down. The holes appeared to me to have been made by stacking the wings together and firing through them, not while in flight. There was a report in the *Houston Chronicle* on October 12, 1996, stating that U-2 pilot, Gary Powers was not downed by Soviet gunfire in 1960 as reported by the Russians. Recently a former Soviet jet fighter pilot revealed that it was the force of the slipstream from his plane that caused Powers' plane to crash!

** The humility of being introduced to, and engage in conversation with, Margaret Thatcher, the former prime minister of England, at a function in The Houston Club.

** The satisfaction of buying futures in ten cases of 1982 LaFite Rothschild for $500 a case and, in 1996, seeing its value reach $4,000-plus a case.

** The wonder of sitting in my aisle seat, in front of the mach meter, on the Concorde flying to Paris from New York and watching the dial approach and arrive at Mach 2. Just think of it: traveling at 1,088 feet a second or approximately 1,500 miles an hour. At that speed, in one hour, I could leave Houston and be at my home in Palm Desert, California. About halfway there, we could wave "hello" to El Paso as we flew by.

** Total confidence in the engineers for Aerobus: George Pastor, Don Sullivan, Ben Lamoreaux, Wolfgang Bamberg, Andre' Pugin and all of his staff.

** Nausea from the overwhelming smell of rotting fish, out of the clear blue, on a native island in Alaska. One of the natives had robbed the fish wheel, brought the fish home, cleaned and hung them on a clothes line and thrown the remains to his dogs. Mrs. Parks has not eaten salmon since the day we experienced that odor. I only eat smoked salmon.

** The puzzlement of one of the strangest incidents in all of my years of having an office. In response to my request to have her make coffee daily, an employee wrote me the following excuse for why she could not:

> "After my conversation with my doctor yesterday afternoon, I was told that I should wait a month to see if it is only my birth control pills causing my upset stomach. She (her doctor) also said that until there is a definite cause, to stay away from anything that might cause nausea."

Upon reading the note, I knew I had lived too long because I thought I had heard of everything — but, obviously, I hadn't.

** There is no range of emotions equal to what you feel, as you sit in anticipation, and the verdict of the jury is handed from the bailiff to the judge and then read aloud.

** Daily, for some years, I have worn a miniature Sweetheart rose in my lapel, behind which is a tiny glass hand blown vase that contains water permitting the rose to stay fresh most of the day.

The flowers are pink and about the size of one's little fingernail. Mrs. Parks and I grow our own roses and I wear the buds always, even in the lapel of a sports jacket. They speak to me of style, and the finishing touch.

** I cannot measure the pride I feel at having been an undergraduate at so eminent an institution as Rice University, and being able to make a small contribution to its future.

** Among my blessings, I count such friends as Betty and Fred Hardy, with whom Mabel and I have shared Thanksgiving and Christmas dinner for years.

I still believe there is an American dream . . . and I have experienced it.

SOURCES

In addition to the author's own files and recollections, background material for the di Portanova estate case, in Chapter 5, was drawn from a richly detailed article in the March 1982 issue of *Texas Monthly*, "The Very Rich Life of Enrico Di Portanova," by John Davidson.

In describing the early history of the Indian Territory and Oklahoma statehood, in Chapter 1, two books were used as references: *Oklahoma — A History of Five Centuries,* by Arrell Morgan Gibson; and *Closing the Frontier,* by John Thompson, both published by the University of Oklahoma Press.

Special photos by Jace Ray. All other photographs are from the personal collection of Fred Parks.

Index

280